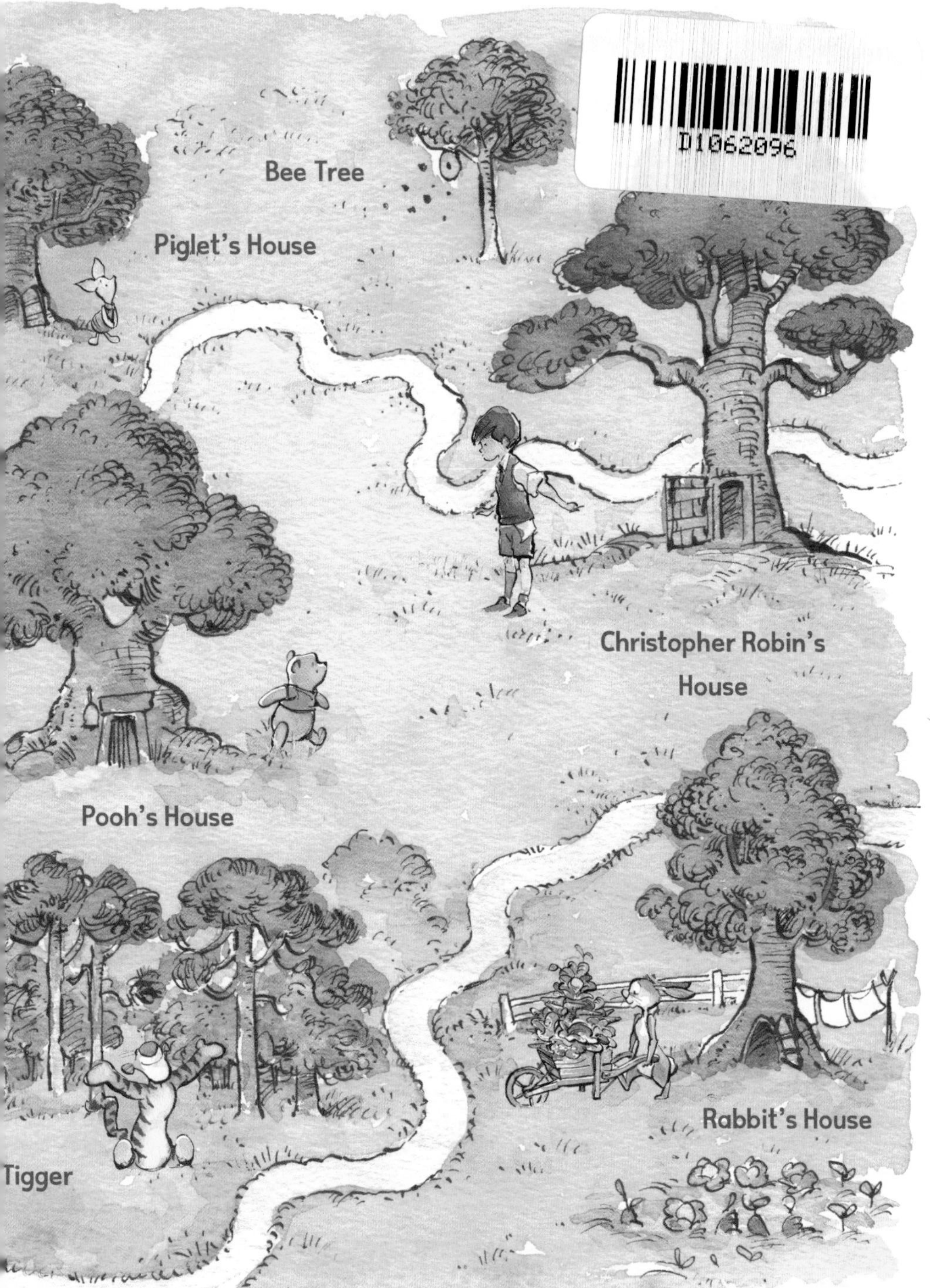
Bee Tree
Piglet's House
Christopher Robin's House
Pooh's House
Rabbit's House
Tigger

95
YEARS
Disney
Winnie the Pooh

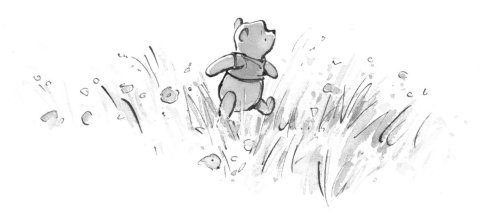

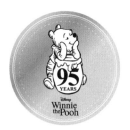

Based on the "Winnie the Pooh" works by A. A. Milne and E. H. Shepard

For information address Disney Editions, 1200 Grand Central Avenue,
Glendale, California 91201.

Library of Congress Control Number: 2020949975
ISBN 978-1-368-07609-8
FAC-034274-21204

Printed in the United States of America
First Hardcover Edition, September 2021
10 9 8 7 6 5 4 3 2 1
Visit www.disneybooks.com

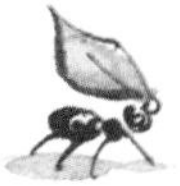

For Linus and Verity

—Aunt Cathy

For Connor, this one's for you.

—Mike

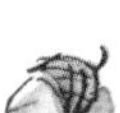

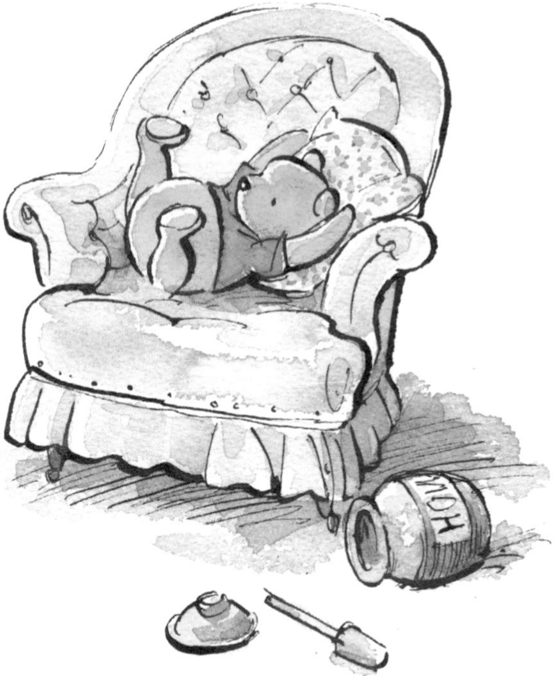
HUNNY

The little things in life

words by Catherine Hapka

pictures by Mike Wall

Disney EDITIONS

New York • Los Angeles

"Hello, new day.

It's lovely to meet you!"

Every new morning is a gift.

"Up, down, touch the ground . . .
I wonder what's for breakfast."

Looking forward to something pleasant

can be pleasant in itself.

"Oh, dear! Where, oh where, might a
hungry bear find a smackerel of honey?"

Why sit at home and curse your empty belly

when a friend might have food to share?

"Christopher Robin, might you have any
honey to spare?"

Being able to ask for help is a strength, not a weakness.

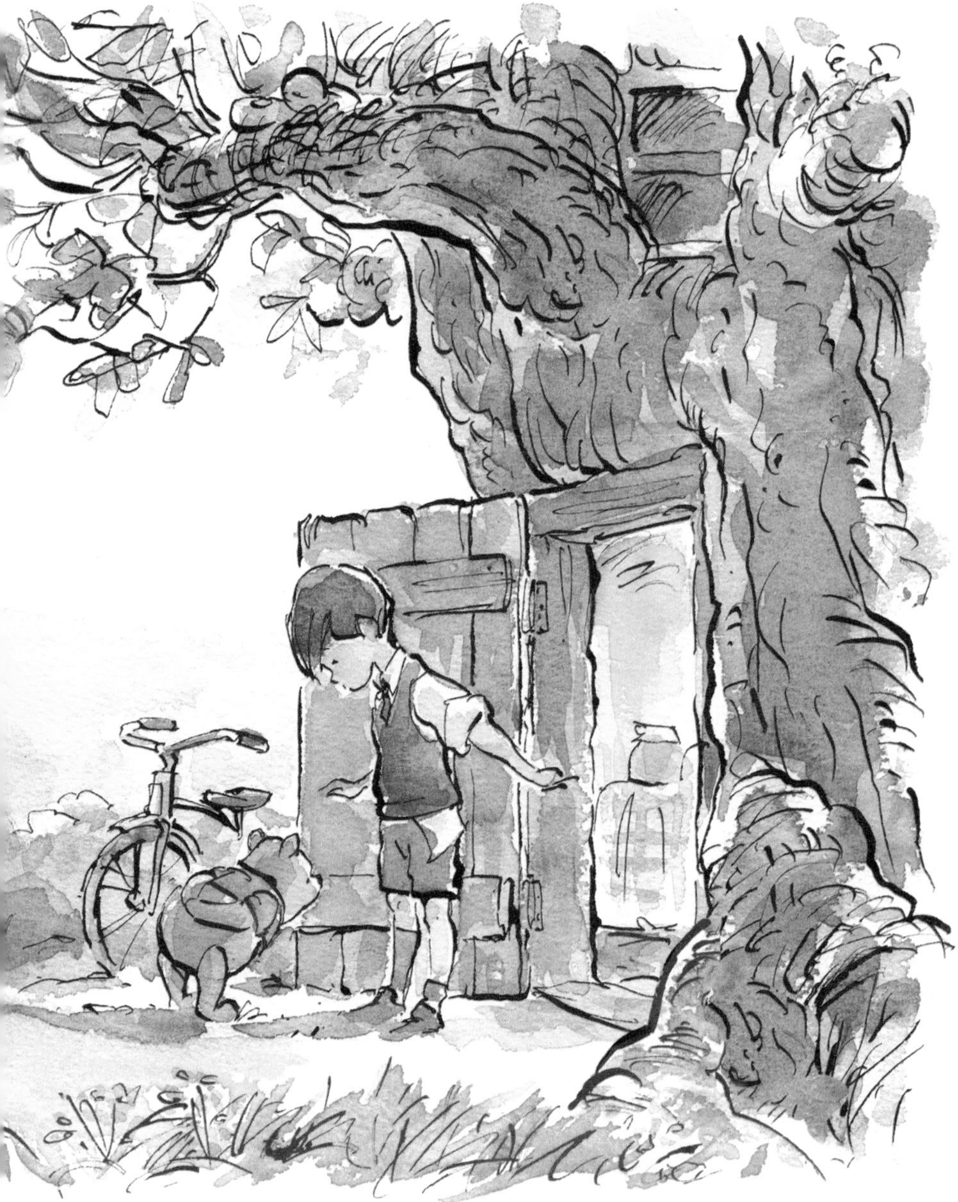

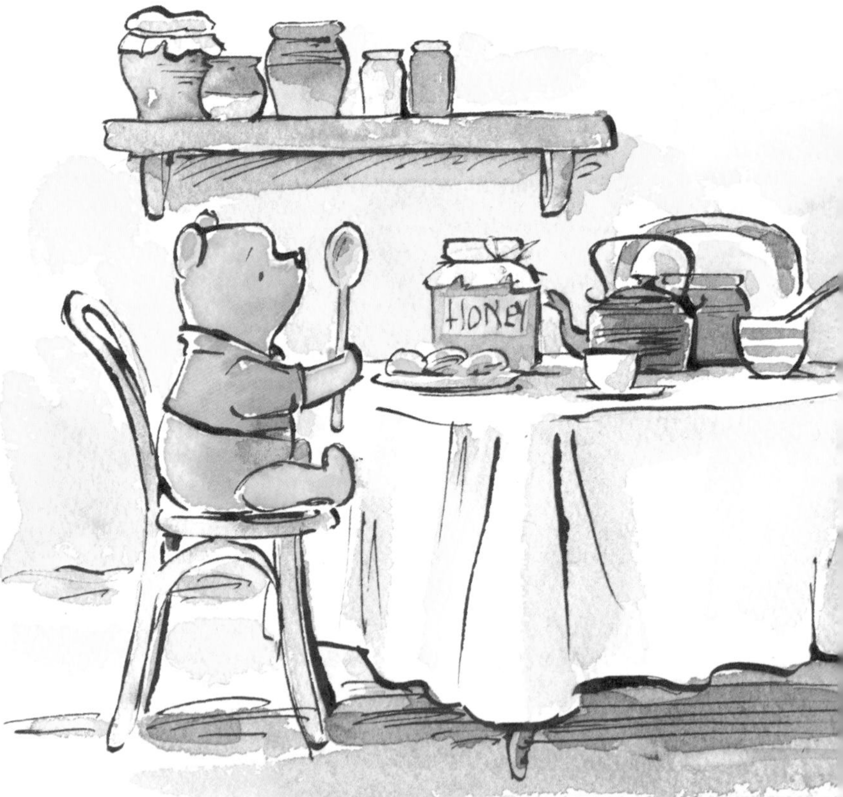
HONEY

"Now, where could my lucky stone have gone?"

A thing need not be valuable to be precious.

"Don't worry, Christopher Robin.

"We'll find it!"

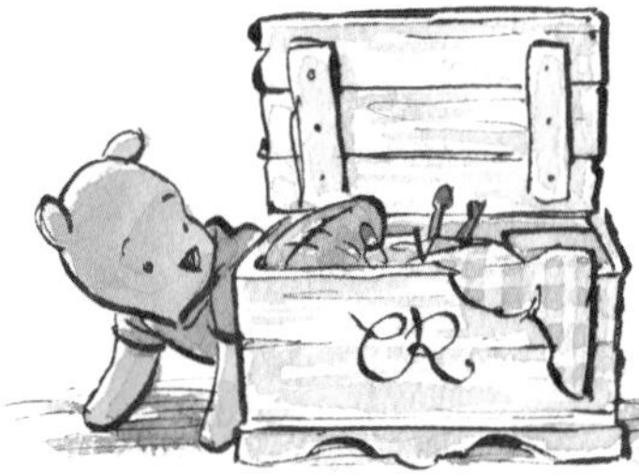
CR

Never wait . . .

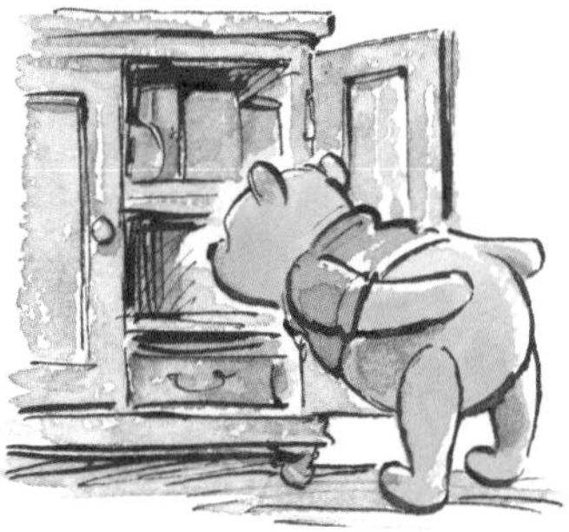

to be asked for help.

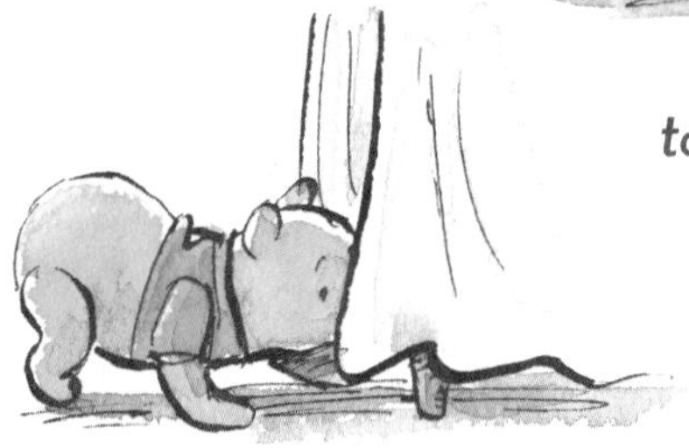

Offer it freely . . .

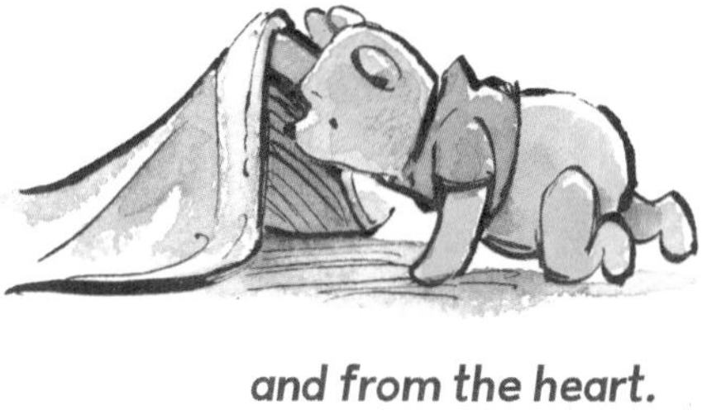

and from the heart.

"It's all right, Pooh Bear. My lucky stone
will turn up. Things generally do."

Strive to understand what is meant,
not only what is said.

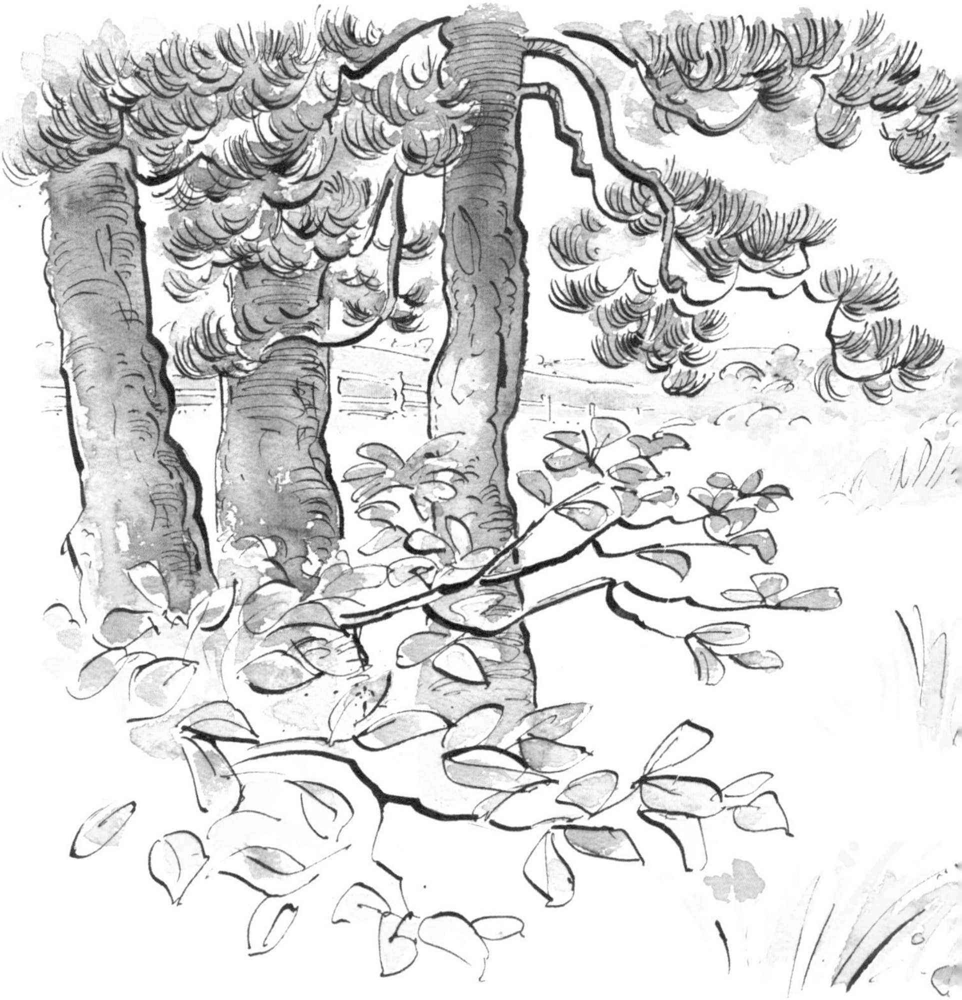

"How can a bear of very little brain find a small but very important lucky stone?"

Questioning yourself can be good.
Doubting yourself rarely is.

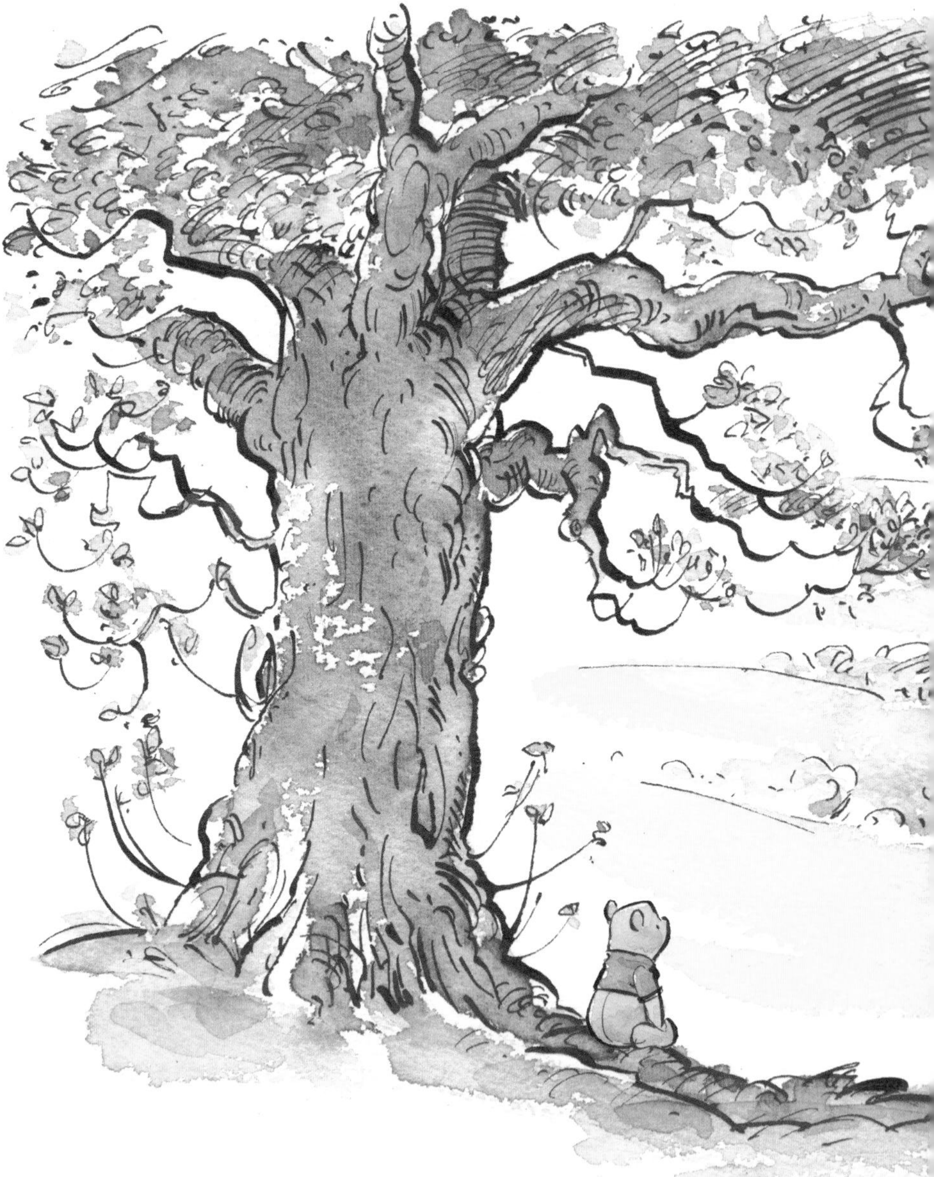

"Think, think, think. . . ."

No moment spent in thought is wasted,

no matter how long or short the moment

or how large or small the thought.

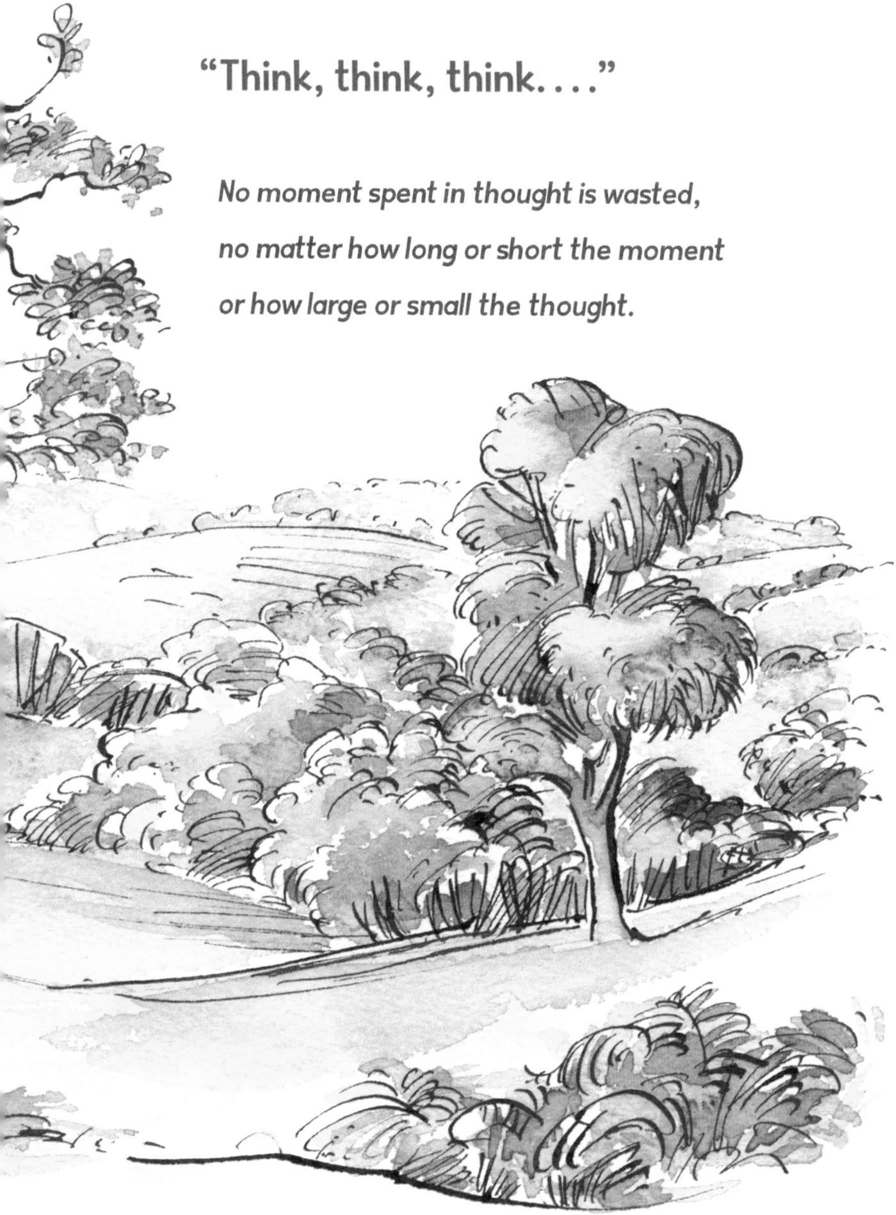

"Where there are bees . . .

Always be aware of the world around you . . .

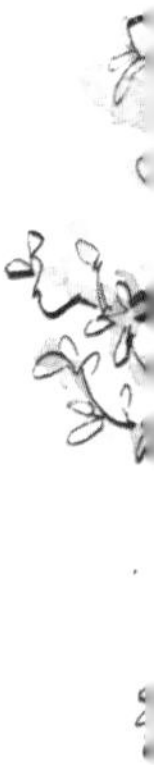

“. . . there is honey!”

. . . for a chance observation can lead to great things.

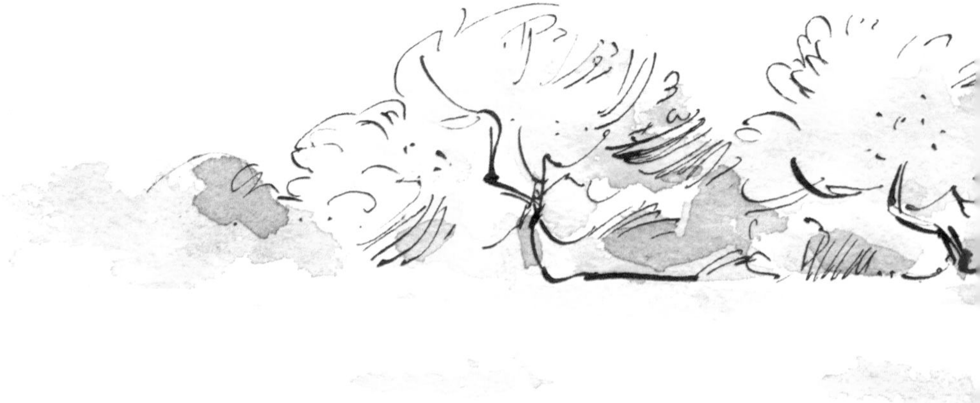

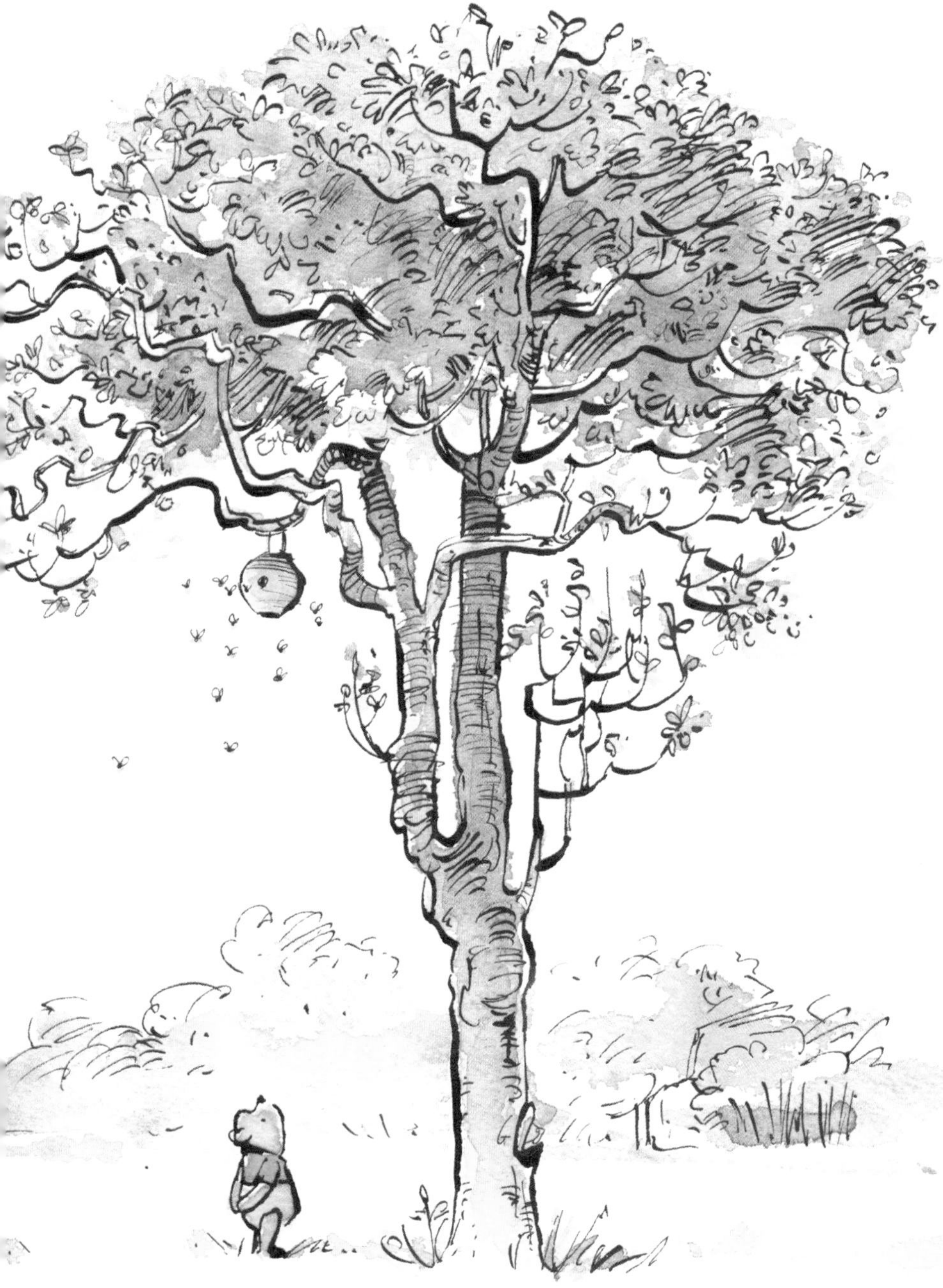

"But the honey wouldn't happen without all the bees helping."

There's nothing like spending a day in nature to remind us that the world is full of miracles.

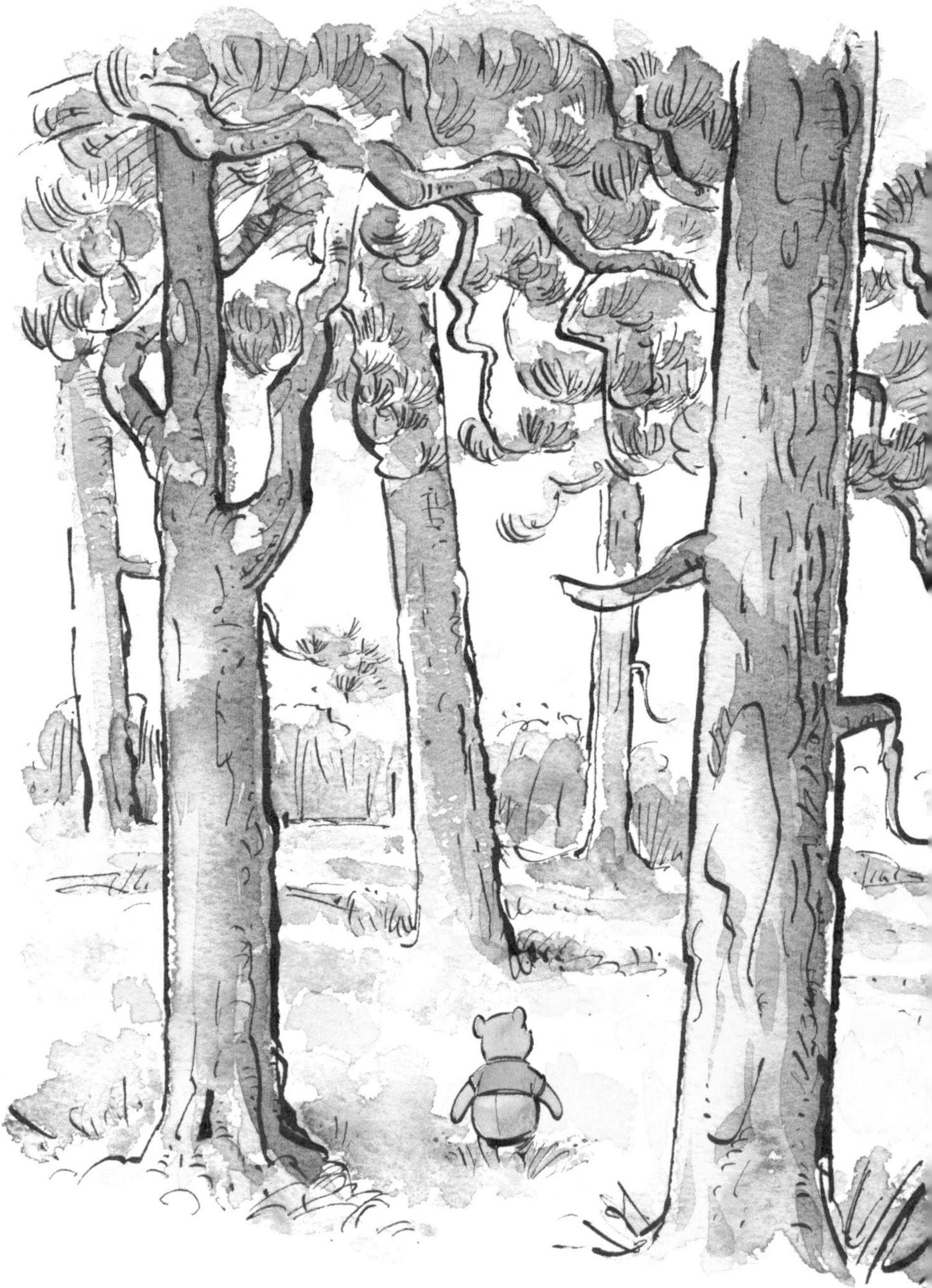

"To help Christopher Robin, I need more bees—er, I mean, friends."

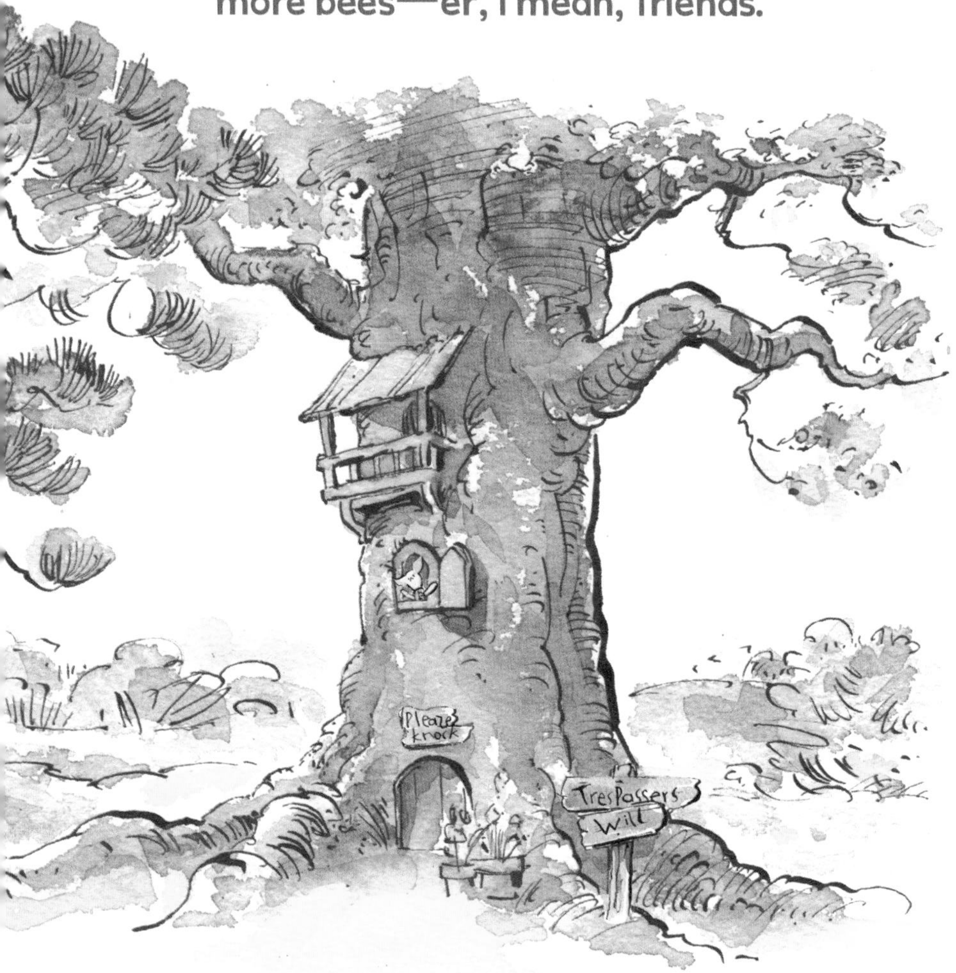
Pleaze knock
TresPassers
Will

Your friends are one of your greatest resources, and you are one of theirs.

"Perhaps a very small friend can help find a very small lucky stone. . . ."

"Of course I'll help, Pooh! Sweeping up can wait."

Don't let minor chores stand in the way of major accomplishments.

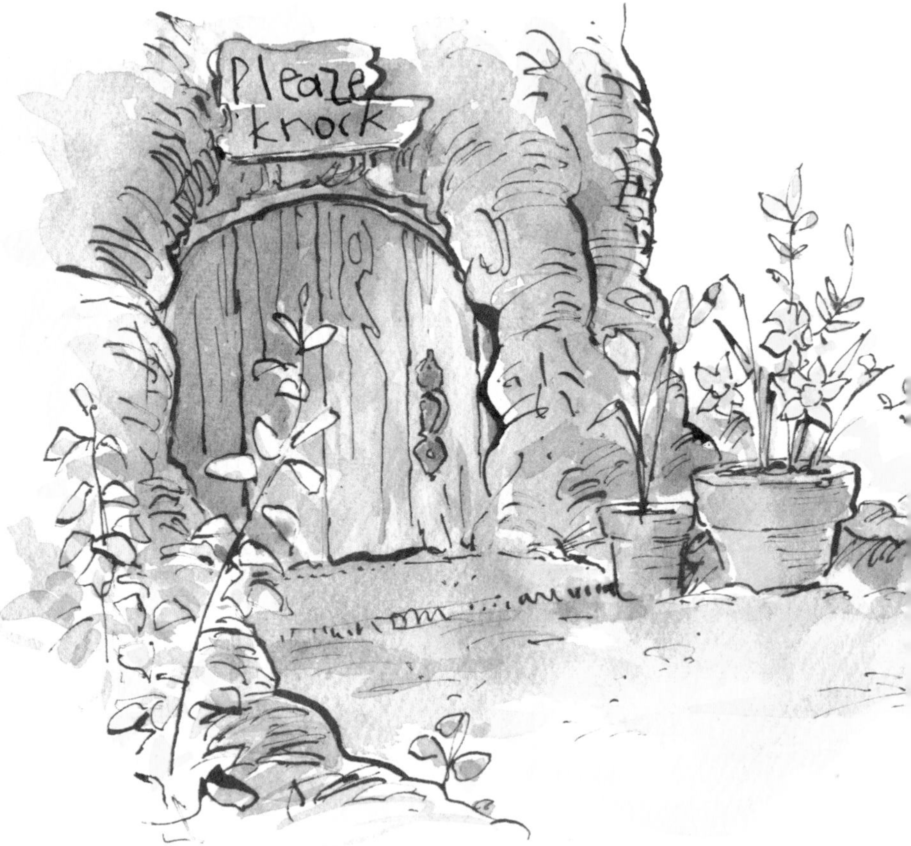
Pleaze
knock

"Is this a quest, Pooh?
It feels quite like a quest."

"I suppose it must be one,
then!"

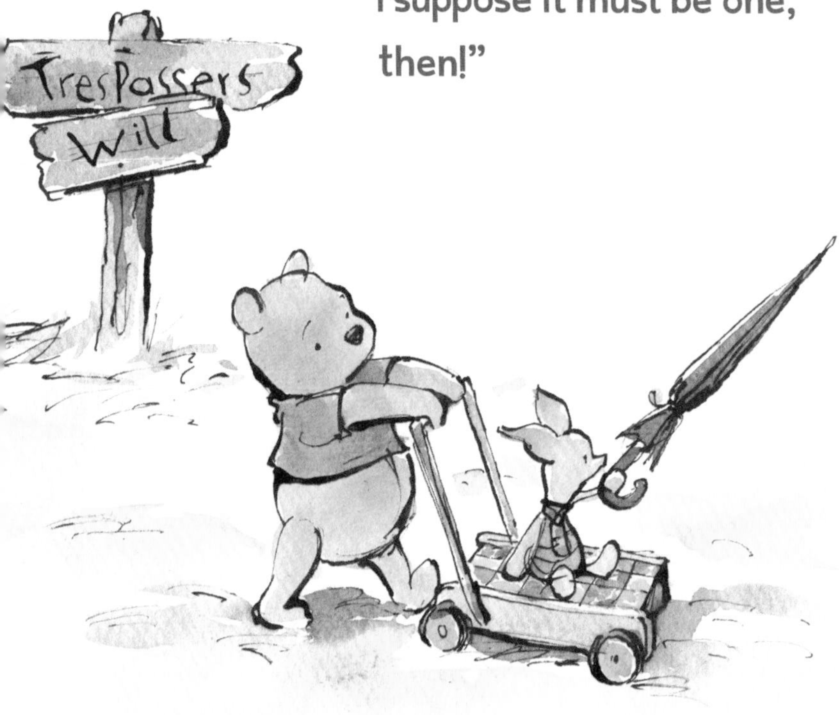
TresPassers
Will

Each new moment is an opportunity for a new adventure.

"Oh, d-d-dear, dear. How will we ever find one special stone among so many?"

"I don't know, Piglet. But we have to try."

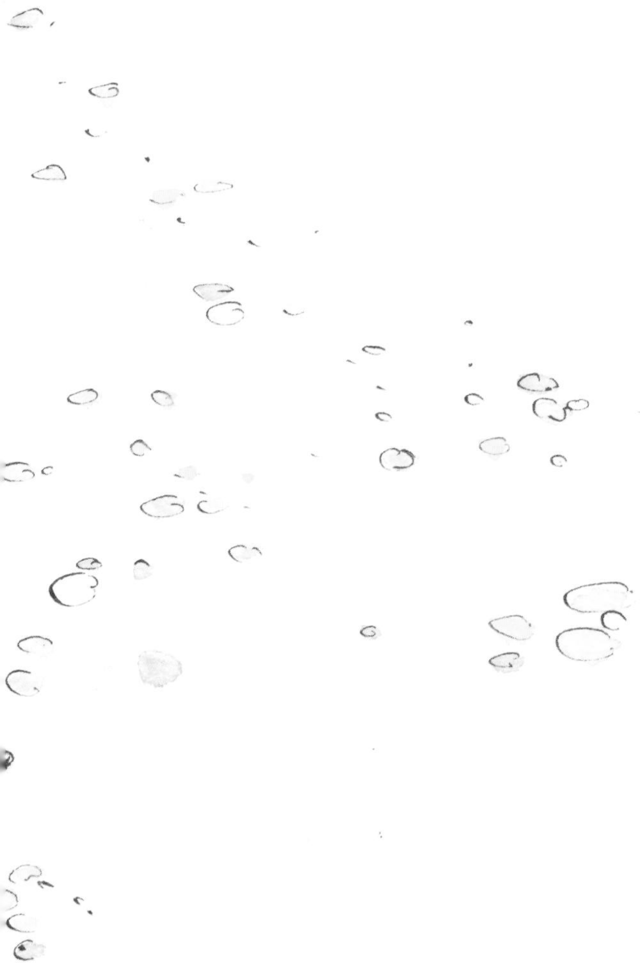

At times life can seem overwhelming. That's when it helps to focus on the little things and just keep going.

"Hoo-hoo-hoo-HOO!
Some bouncin', huh?"

*Life is more fun when you throw yourself
at it wholeheartedly.*

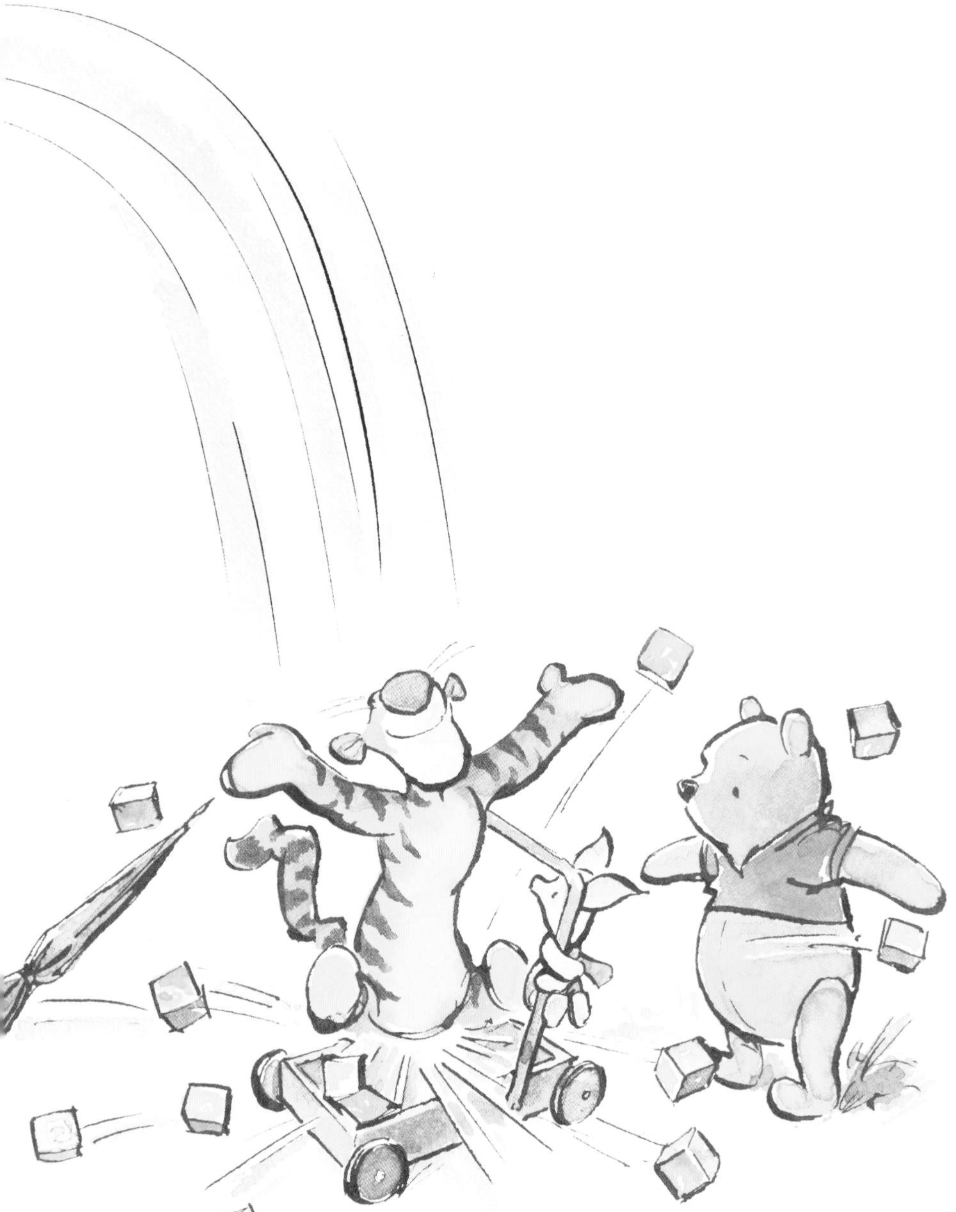

"Will you help us with our quest,
Tigger?"

"Sure thing, Buddy Bear!
Questing's what tiggers do best!"

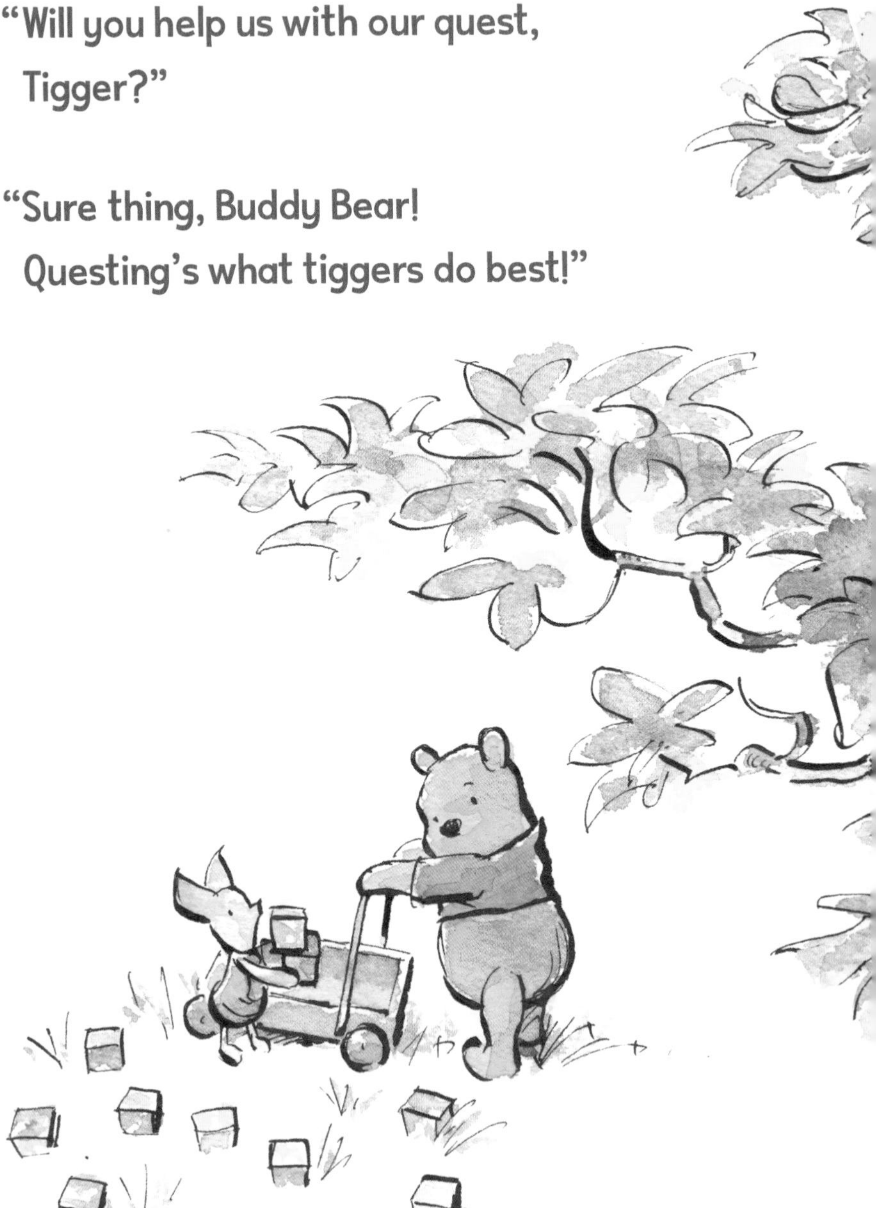

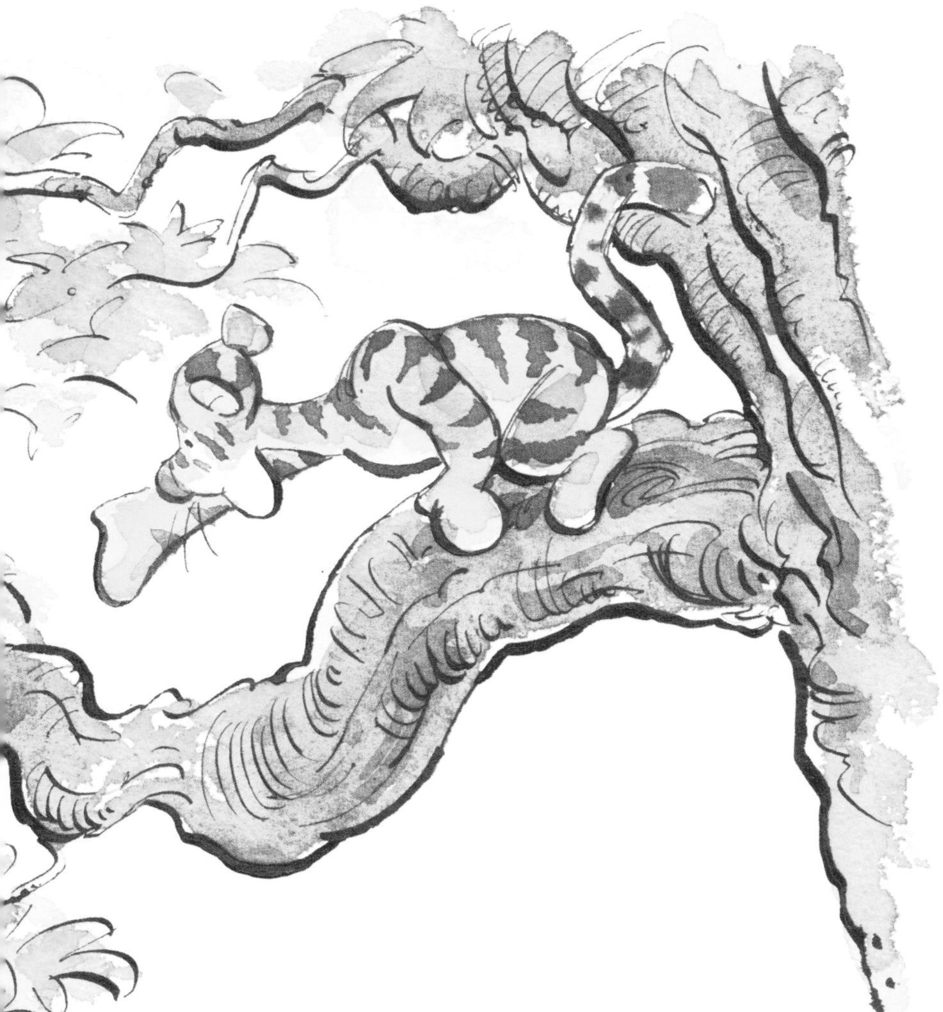

Confidence is contagious!

"Christopher Robin lost somethin',
  huh?

"Is it this?

"Or this?

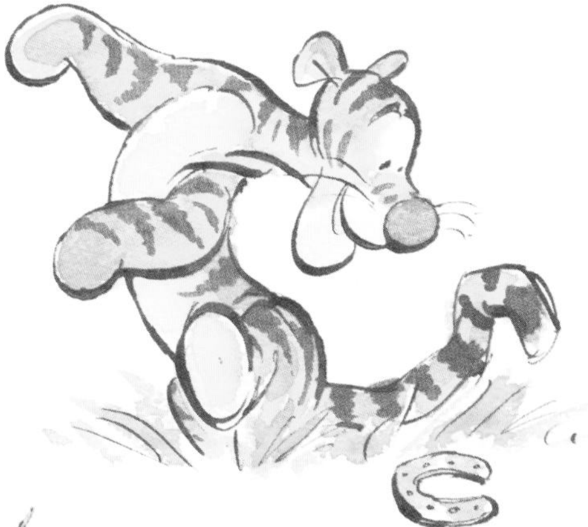

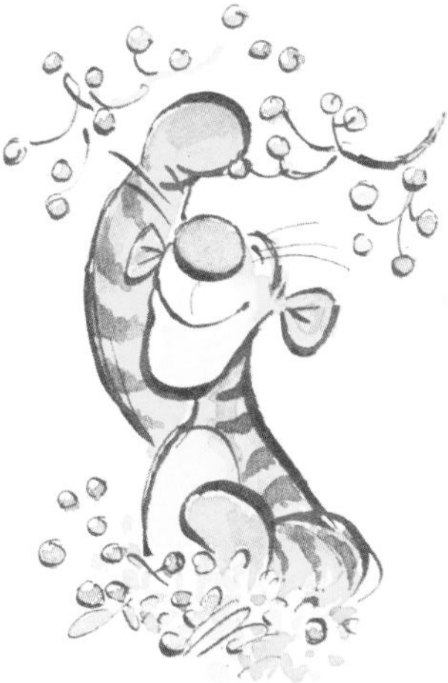

"Gotta be this!"

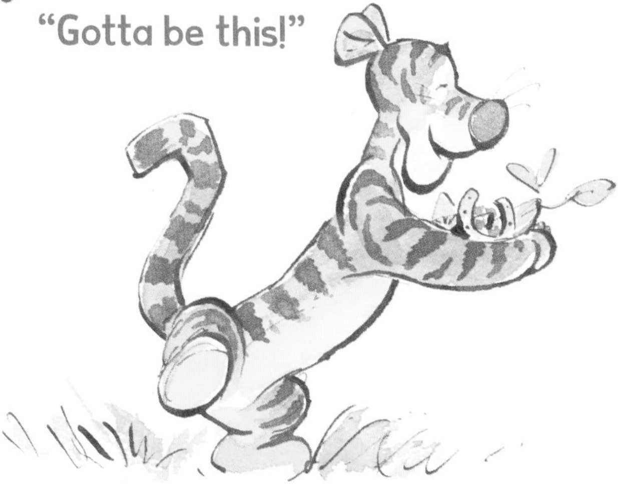

"If anything is worth doing,

do it with all your heart."

—Buddha

"Er, sorry, but I don't think any of these are right, Tigger."

"It's okay, Piglet Ol' Pal. Findin'
'em was fun anyhoo-hoo-hoo-hoo!"

Failure might hold the spark of a future success.

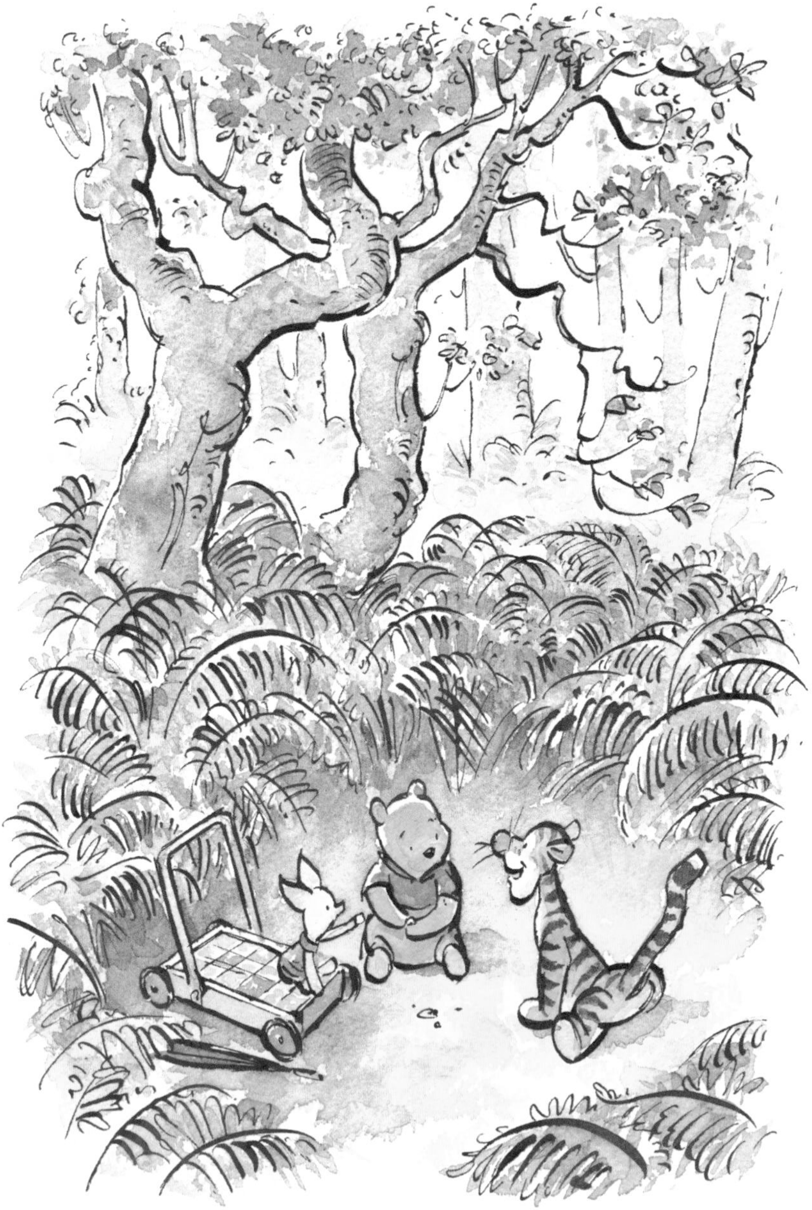

"Oh, d-d-dear. Perhaps this quest
   is too difficult.

"Can we rest and then try again?"

*Take care of your needs and you're
more likely to succeed.*

"Tiggers like questin' better than restin'!"

"Everyone has to rest sometime, Tigger.

"Well, almost everyone."

Take the time to become aware of what surrounds you.

"All this resting has made me
rather hungry."

"I've got an idea, Pooh Boy. . . ."

Try not to let obstacles stand in the way
of your dreams.

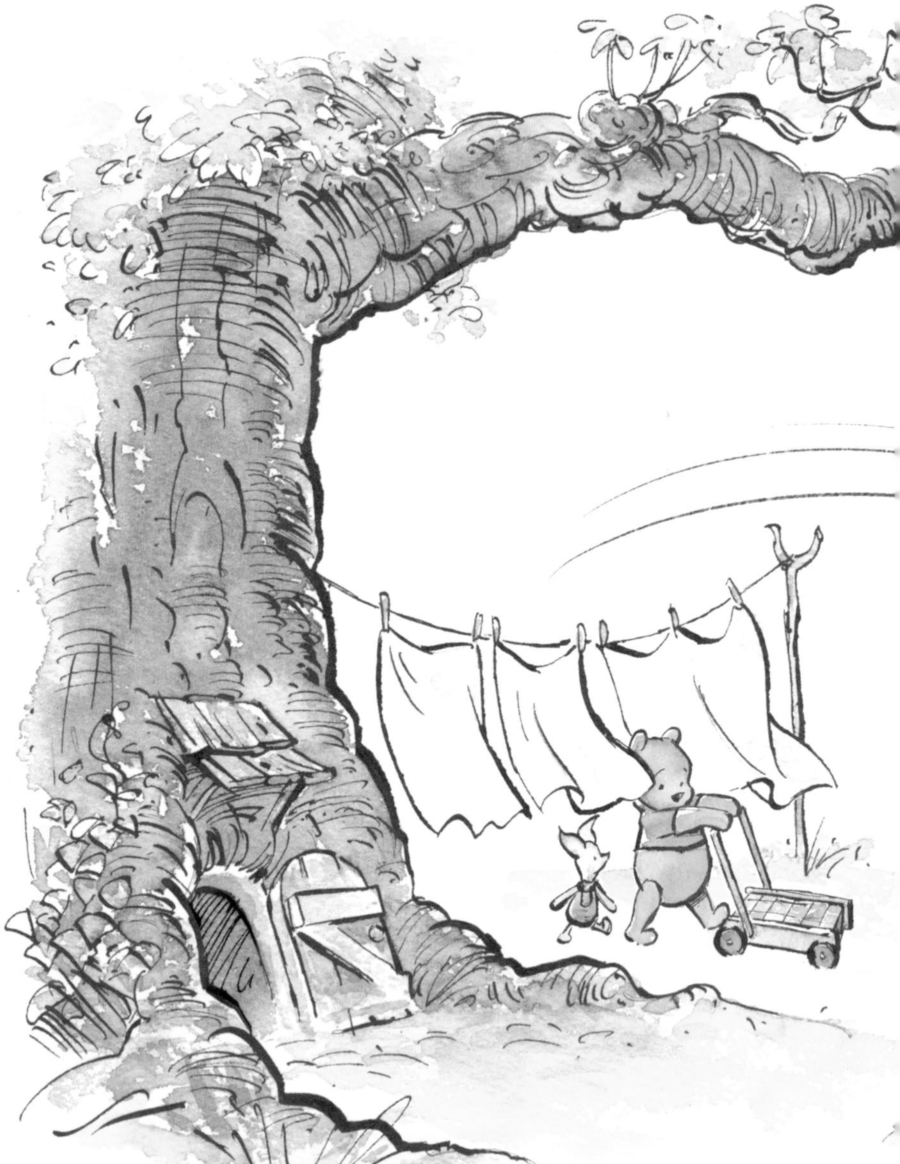

"Hallo, Rabbit! We're here!"

A visit to a friend is always

a cause for celebration.

"I can see that, Tigger . . . especially as you bounced all my radishes out of the barrow!"

Speak your mind and your friends will hear you.

"We'll find your radishes,
   Rabbit!"

"Sure we will, Long Ears.
   We love quests!"

Always take responsibility for your mistakes,
even if you meant no harm.

"Speaking of quests, Rabbit,
   will you join ours?"

"I'd like to help, Pooh.
   But my chores . . ."

Decisions, decisions . . .

Life is full of them.

"We'll help, Rabbit!"

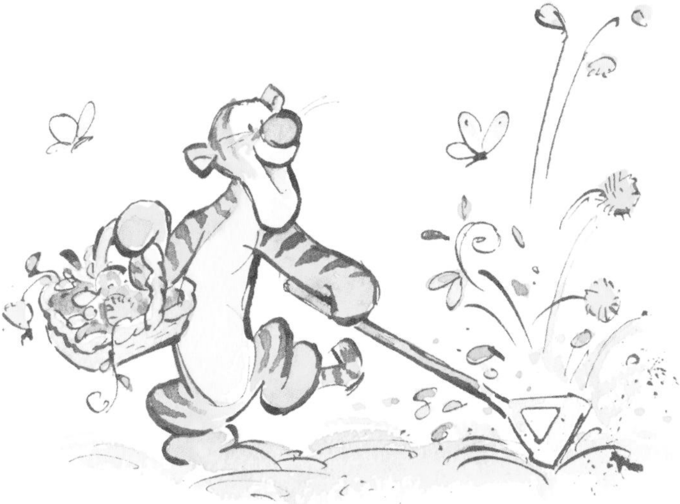

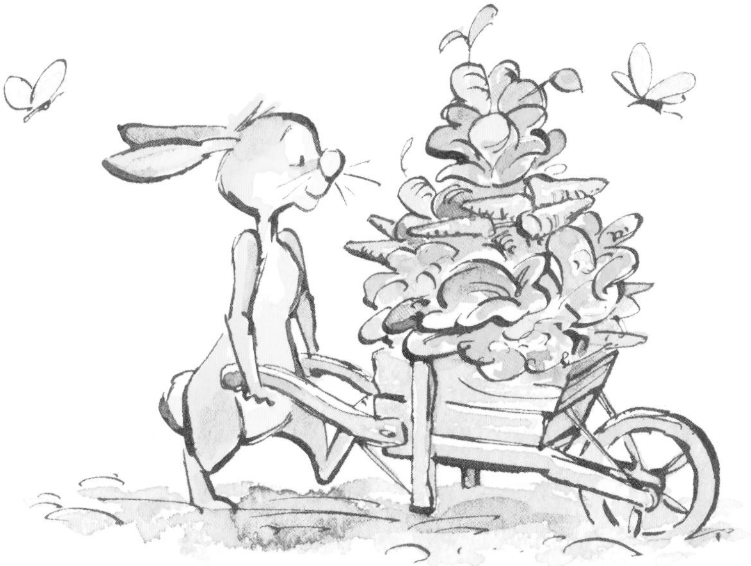

Many hands make light work.

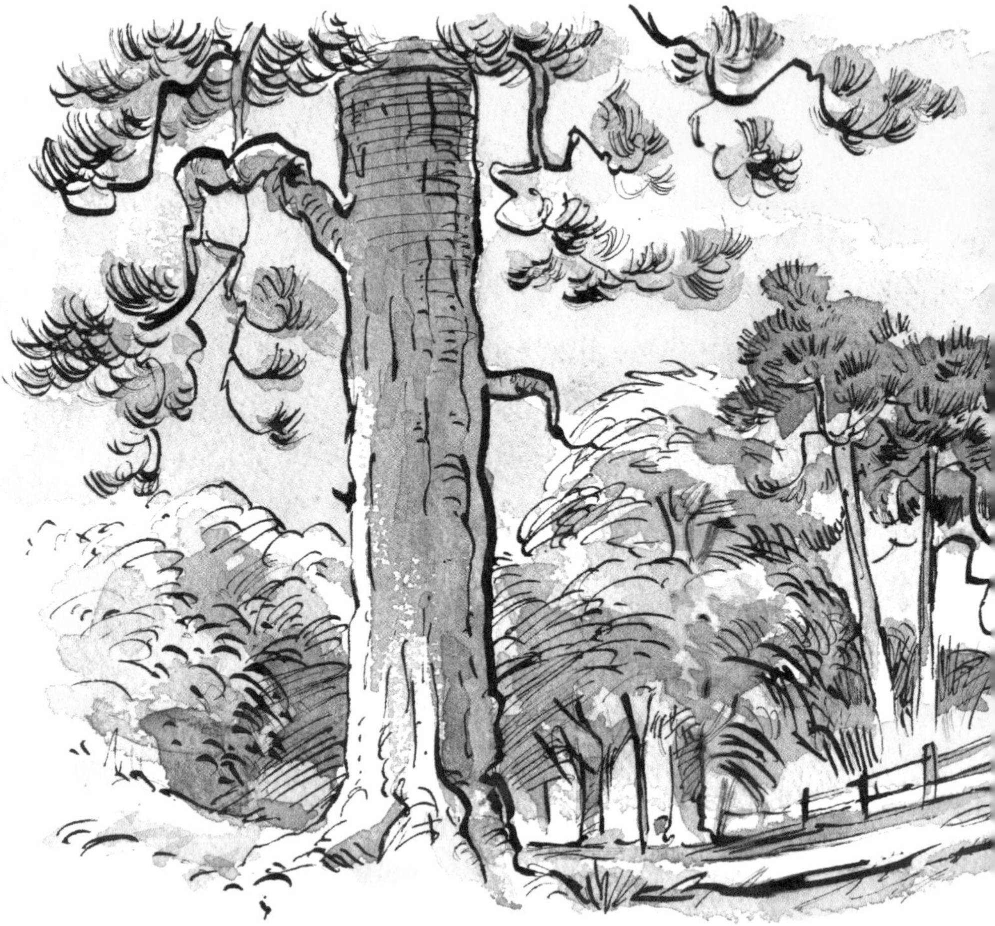

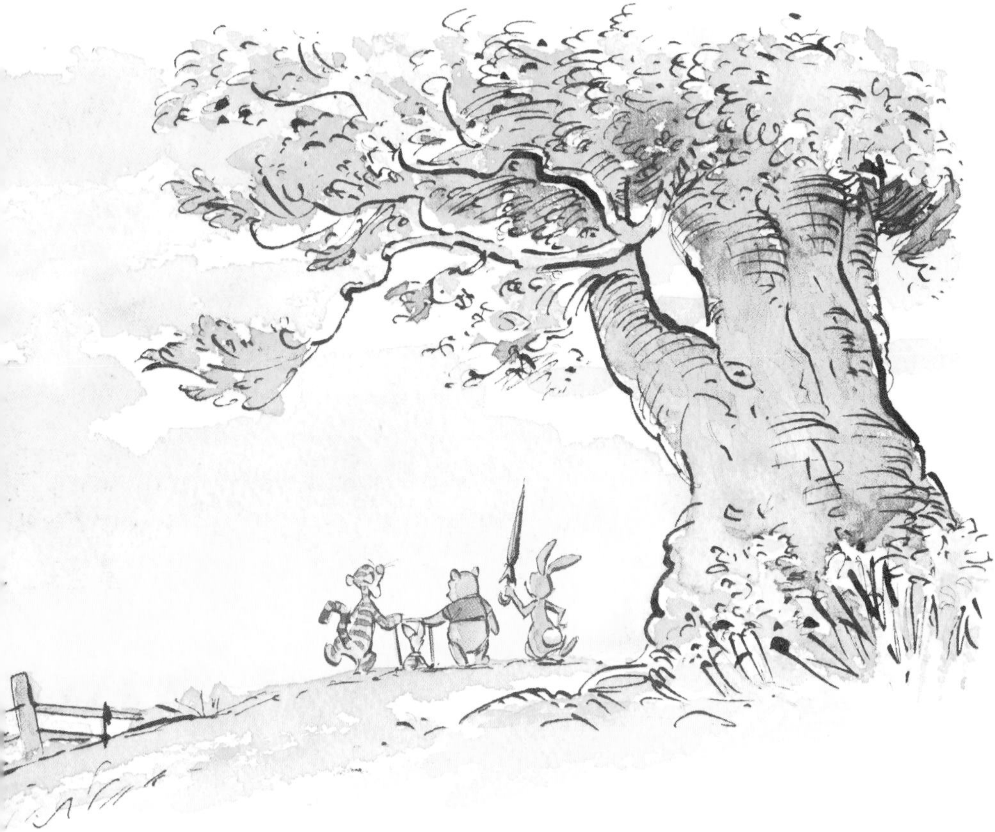

“Off we go!”

"Oh, d-d-dear. It's starting to rain!"

"That's great, little guy. Tiggers love rain!"

Try to appreciate the rain as well as the sun,
the difficult as well as the simple.

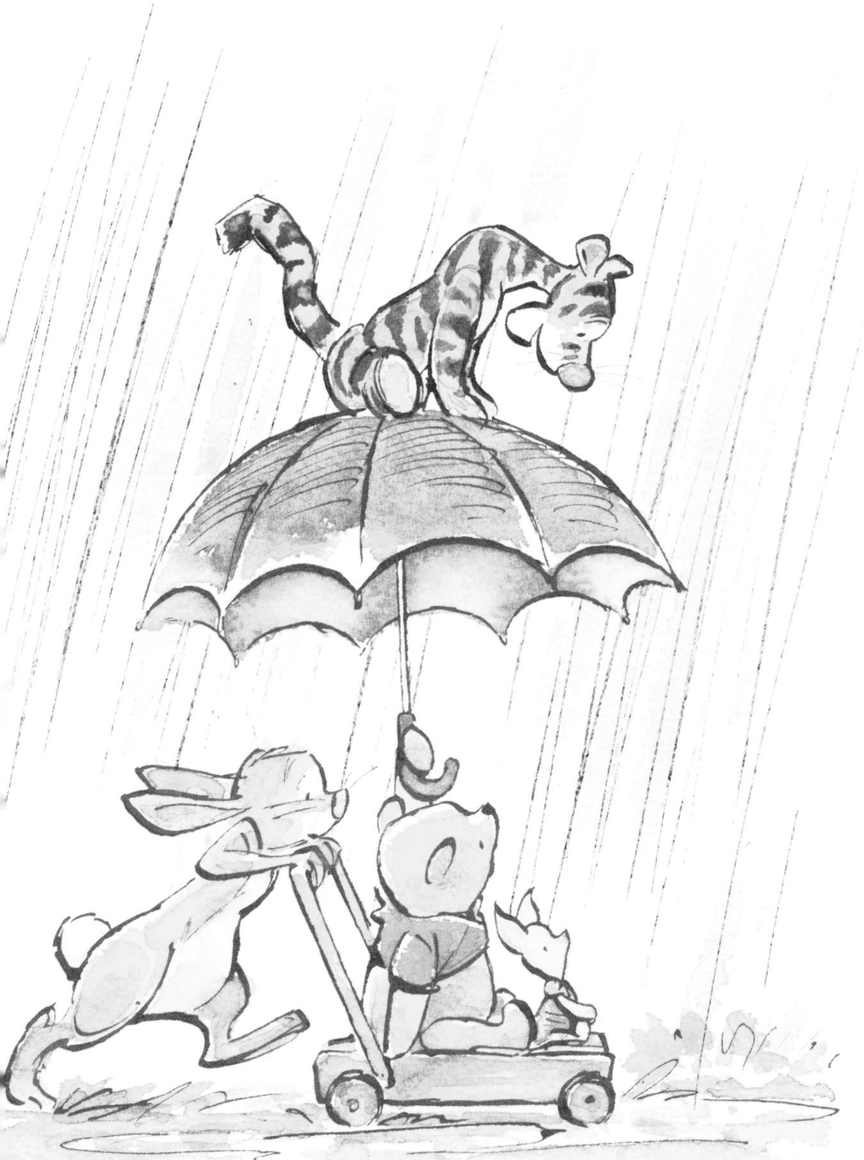

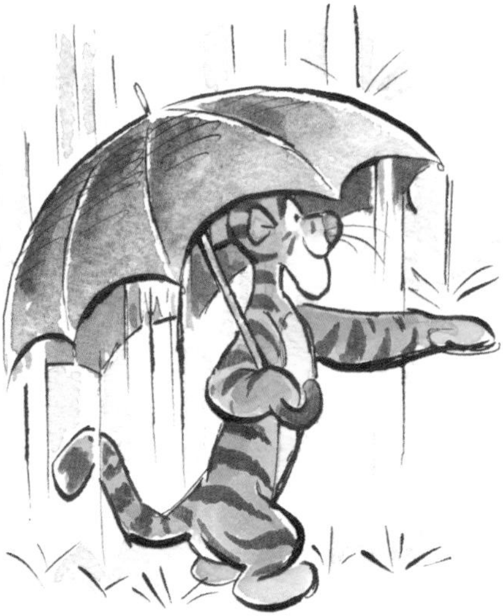
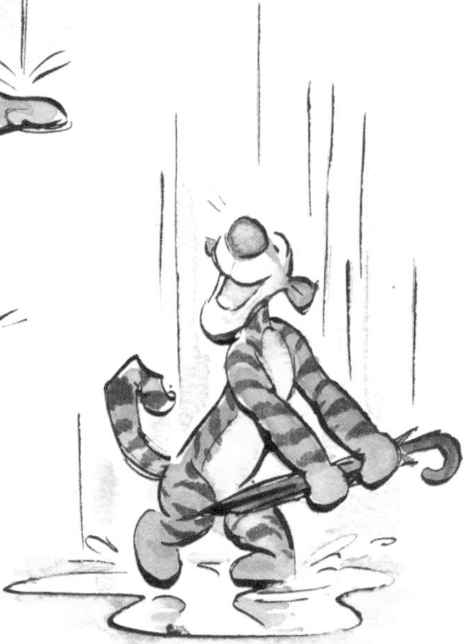
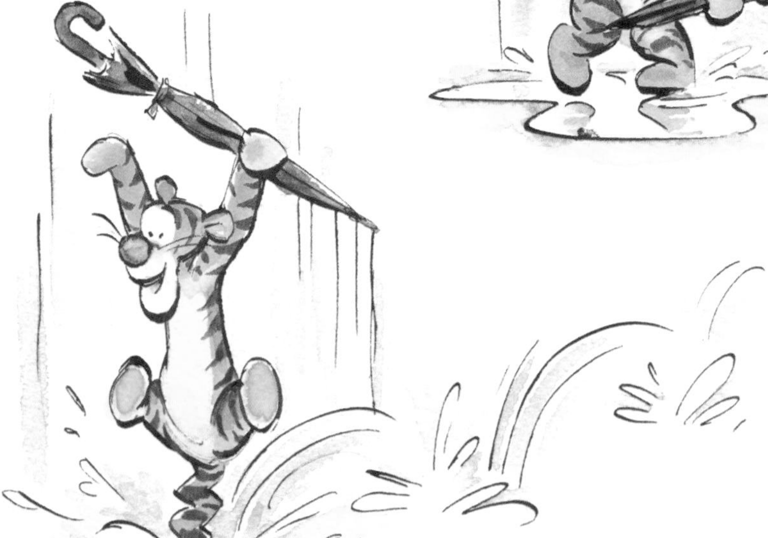

"You're right, Tigger.
   Rain is fun!"

"Told ya, Pooh Boy.
   Fun is what tiggers do best!"

You're never too old to play in rain puddles!

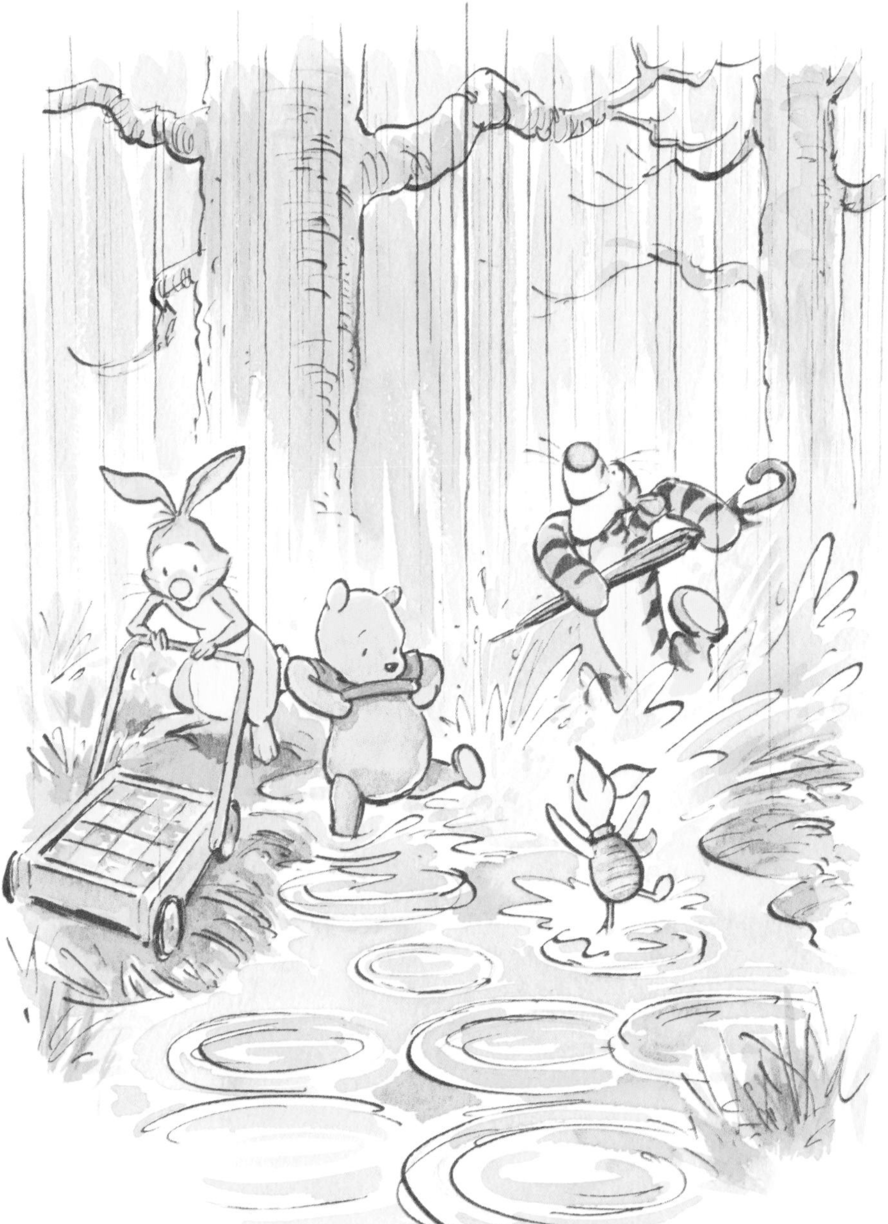

"Do you suppose the rain
will ever stop, Pooh?"

"It has to sometime, Piglet."

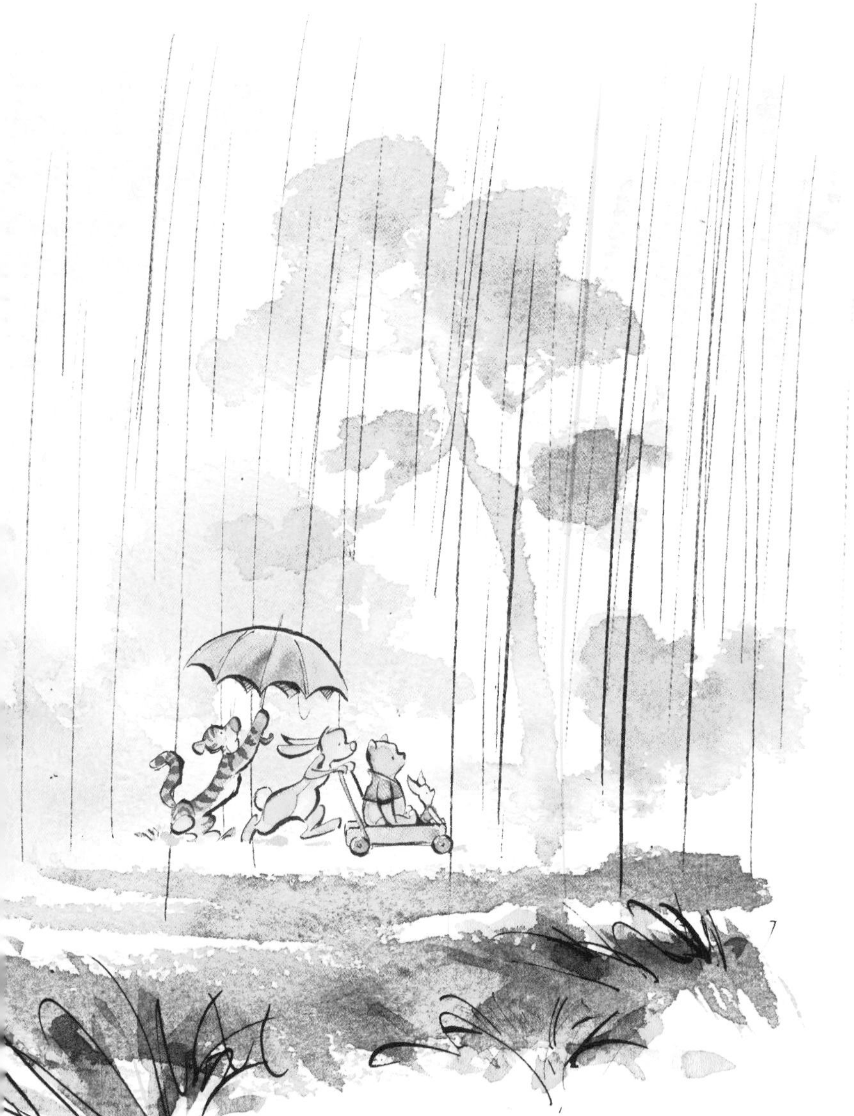

Rain or shine, dark or light,

nothing stays the same forever.

"Tiggers do *not* like
this much rain!"

"Oh, d-d-dear.
I wish it would stop."

"I wish we were somewhere else. . . ."

Consider that some things in life are out of your control.

Somewhere ...

"Nicer."

"Warmer."

"Tastier."

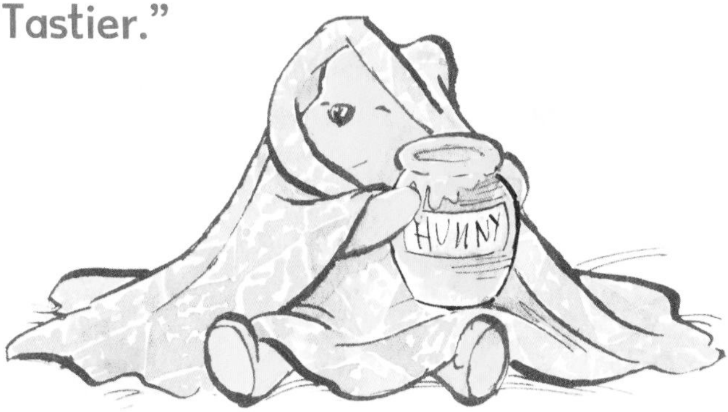
HUNNY

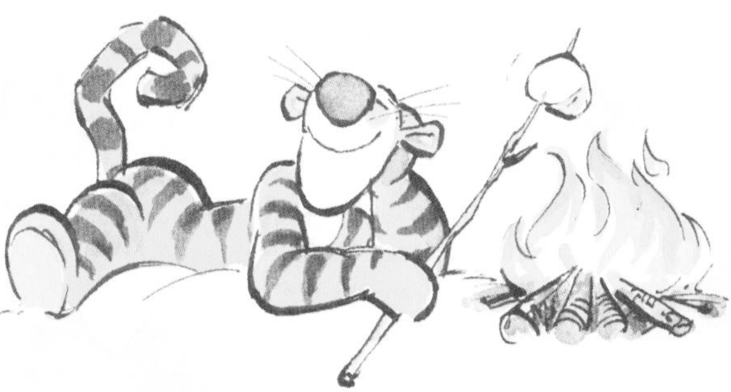

"Toastier."

In dark times, be open to discovering the light.

"Come in, come in!
What are a few drips among friends?"

There is never a bad time to be kind.

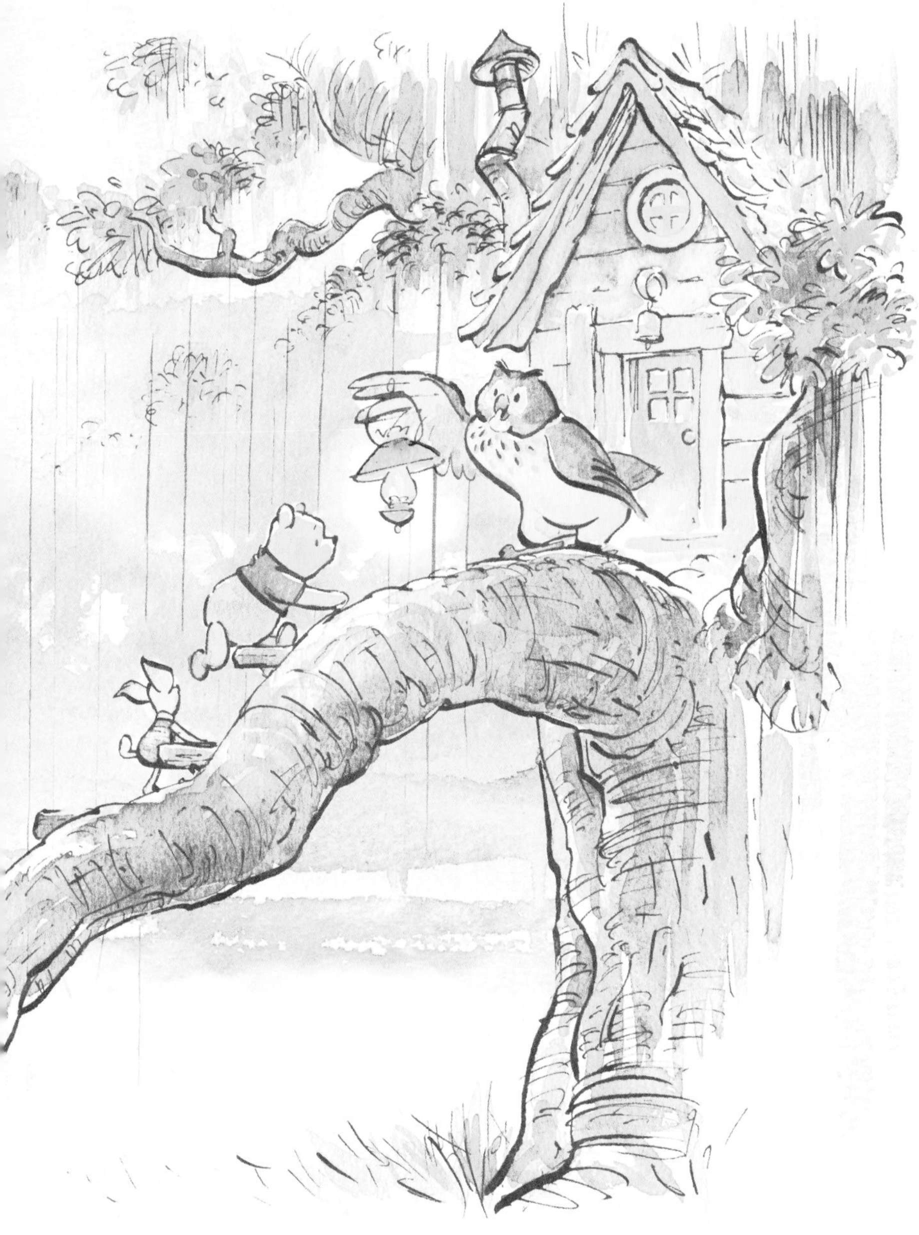

"Thanks, Owl.
 You made our wishes come true!"

"You saved the day, all right, Beak Lips.
 Marshmallow, anyone?"

"Thanks, Tigger.
 I'll have one, please."

"Can I pour you some tea?"

*Little in life is as gratifying
as a gathering of good friends.*

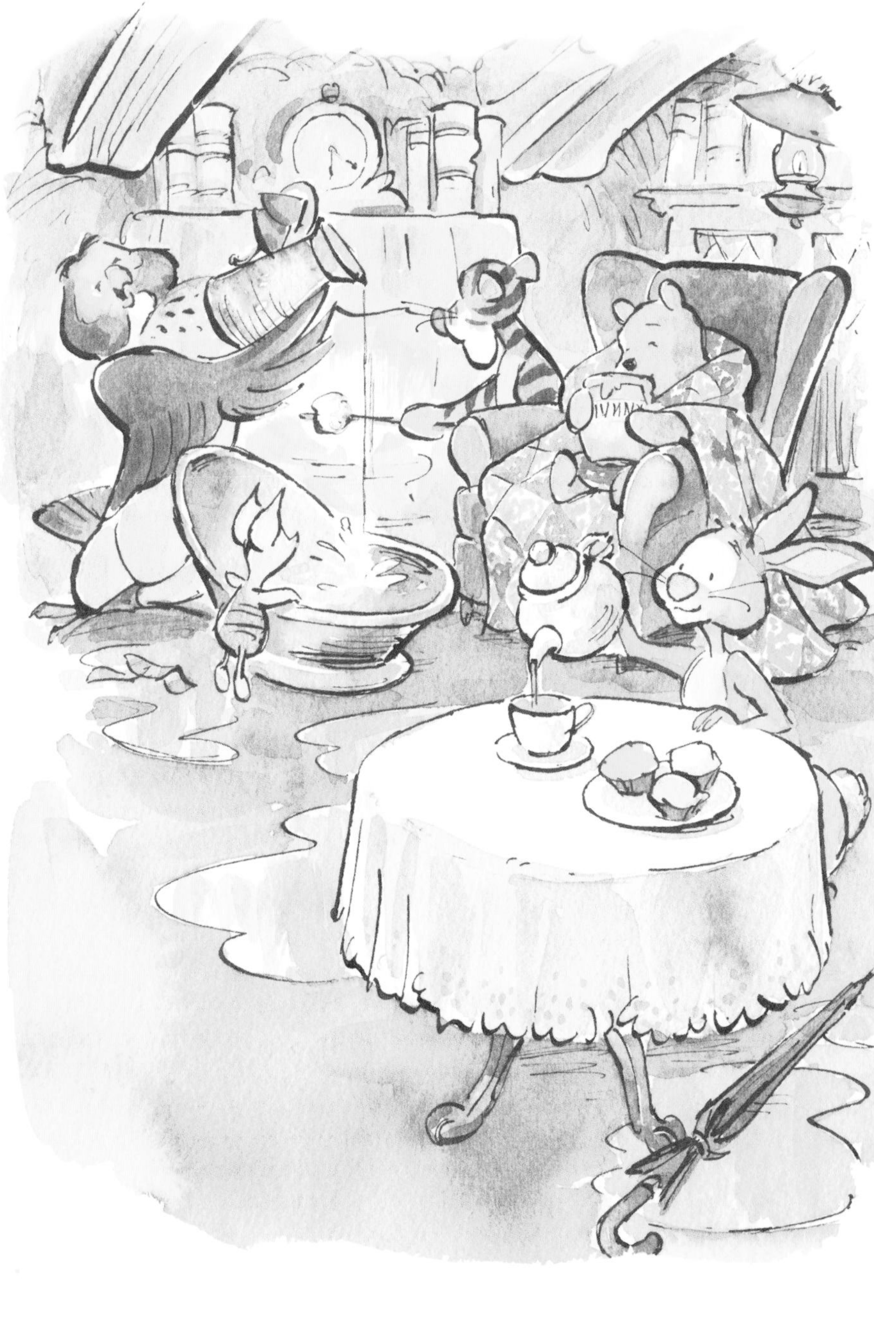

"Is there anything cozier than listening
   to the sound of rain on the roof, Pooh?"

"Yes, Piglet. Doing the same thing
   with good friends."

Cherish every day . . . every moment . . .
every drop of rain . . . and every friend.

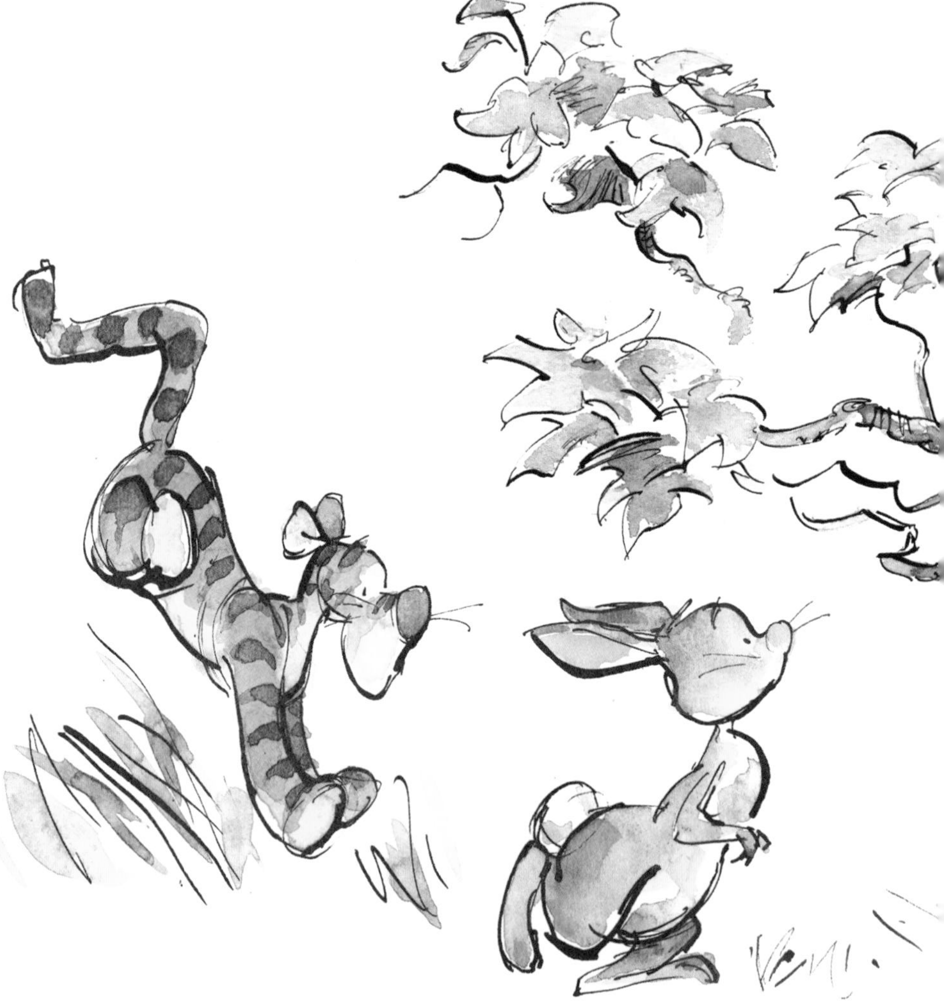

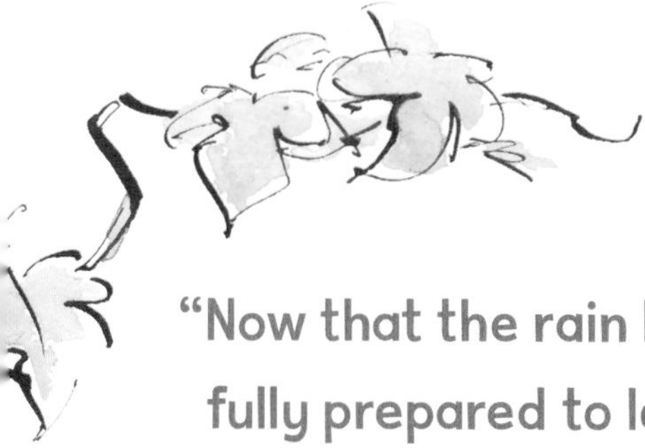

“Now that the rain has cleared, I am fully prepared to lead the quest.

“Good thing I’m here, eh?”

Every leader needs willing followers.

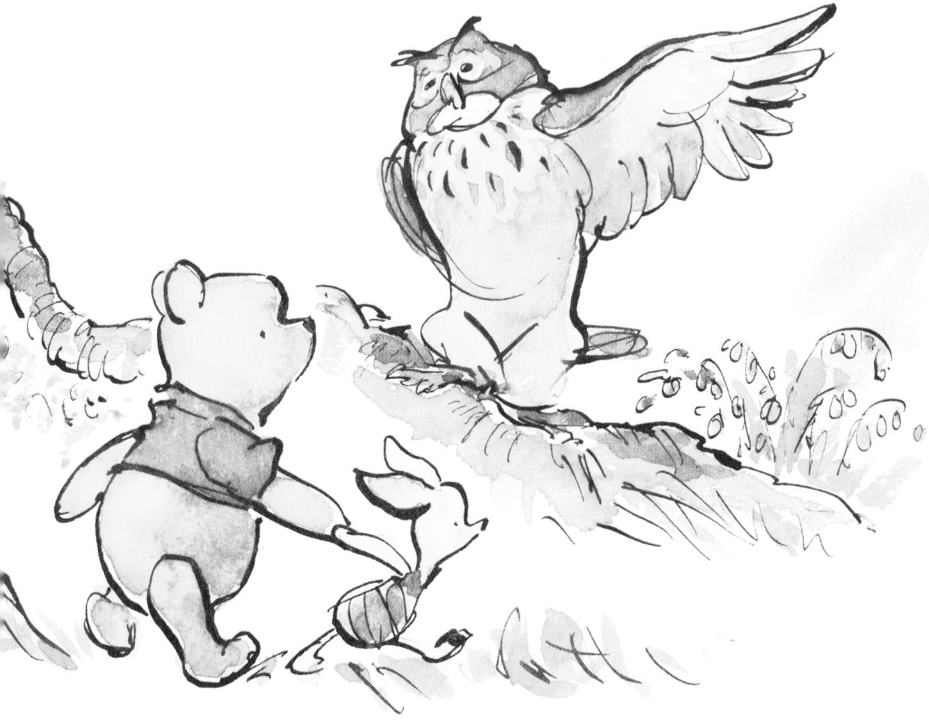

"We're questing after something small, you say? I spy something small just there. Quest solved!"

"Er, Roo is a some*one*, not a some*thing*, Owl."

Whenever you think you have all the answers,

make sure you're hearing the right questions.

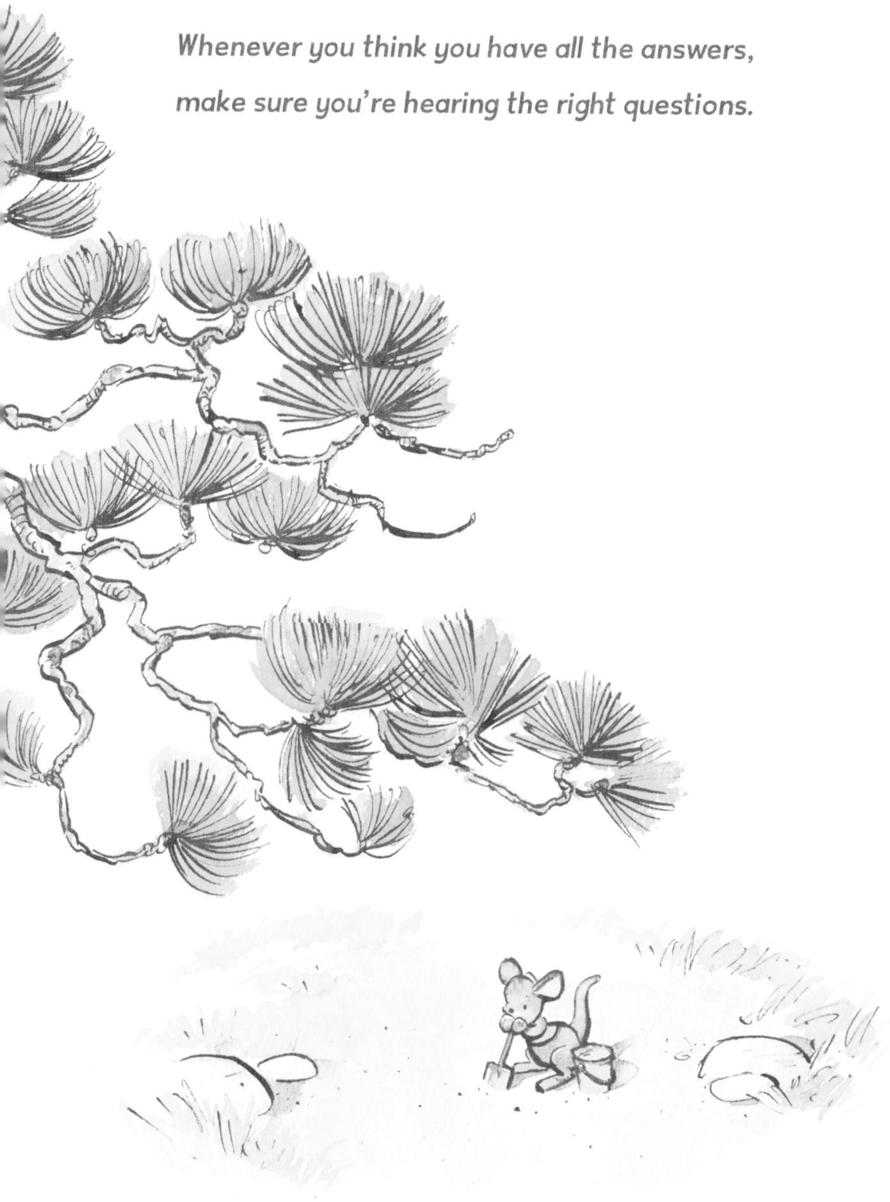

"A quest?
  That sounds like fun!"

"Questing is very serious business,
  young Roo."

"Sure it is, Buddy Bird.
  But it's fun, too!"

A sense of fun is like a pinch of salt—
it can make something good even better.

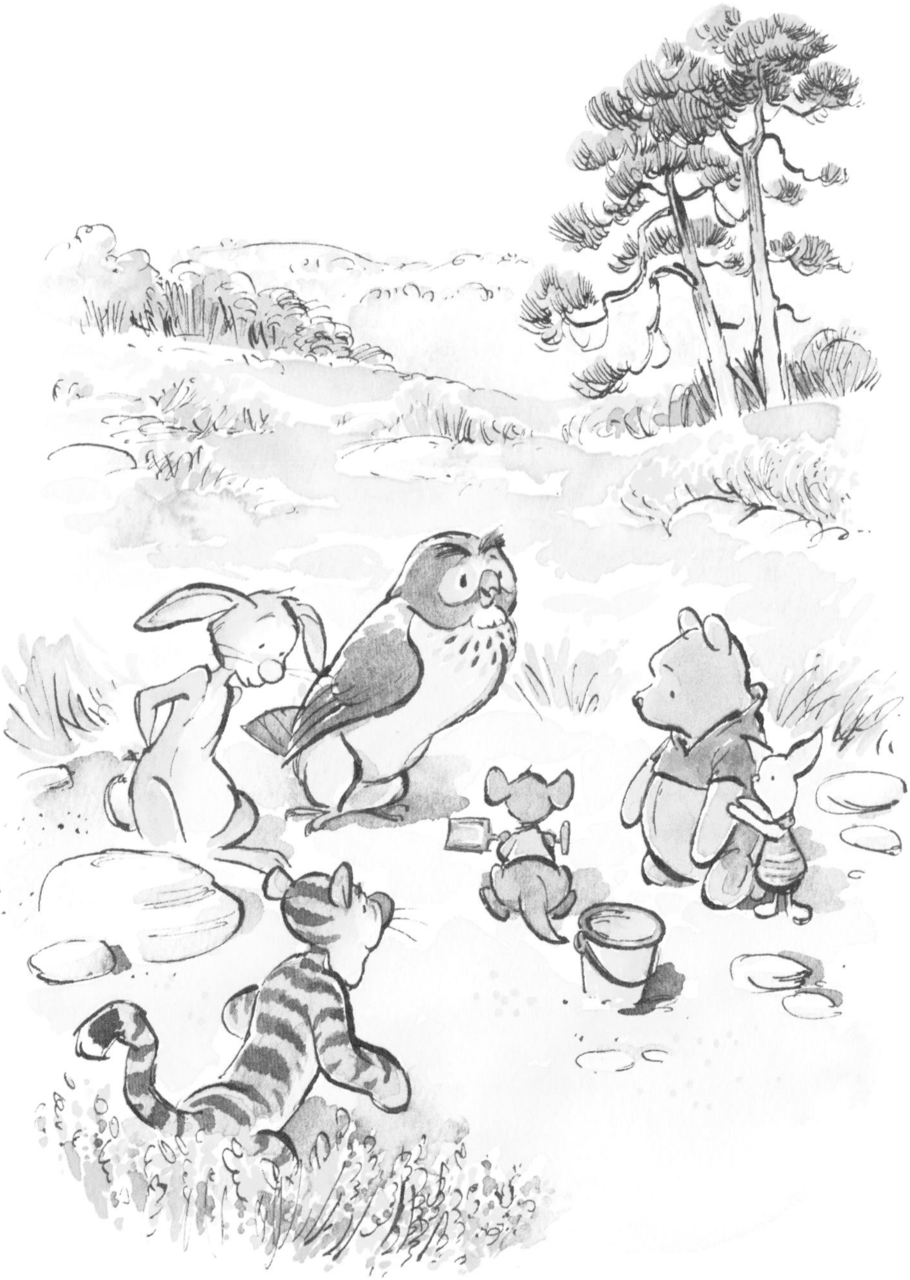

"Mama, may I go?
Please?"

Part of growing up is developing your sixth sense:

a sense of adventure.

"Be careful, Roo!
And good luck with your quest,
everyone!"

It costs nothing to wish someone well.

"Look, here's Eeyore!
Maybe he can help!"

"Thanks for noticin' me, Roo.
Hardly anyone does."

*Be happy to see your friends. You never know what
wonderful memories might be created!*

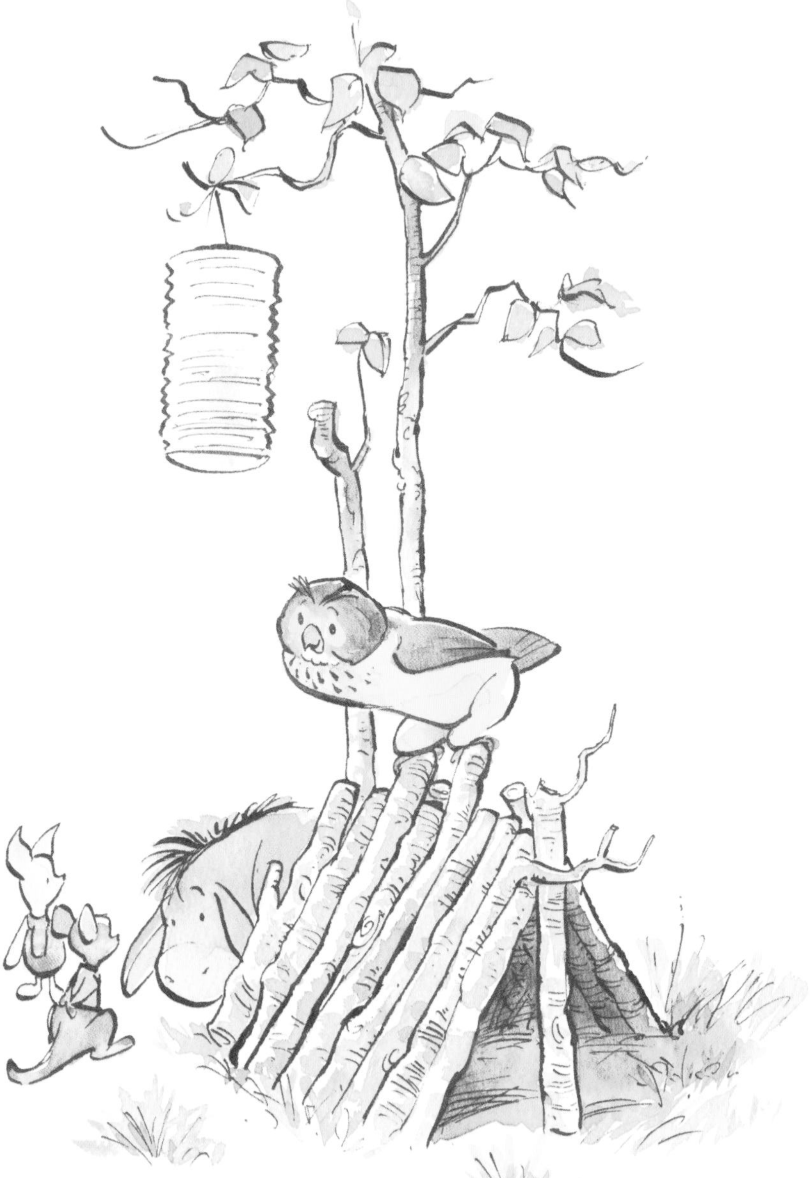

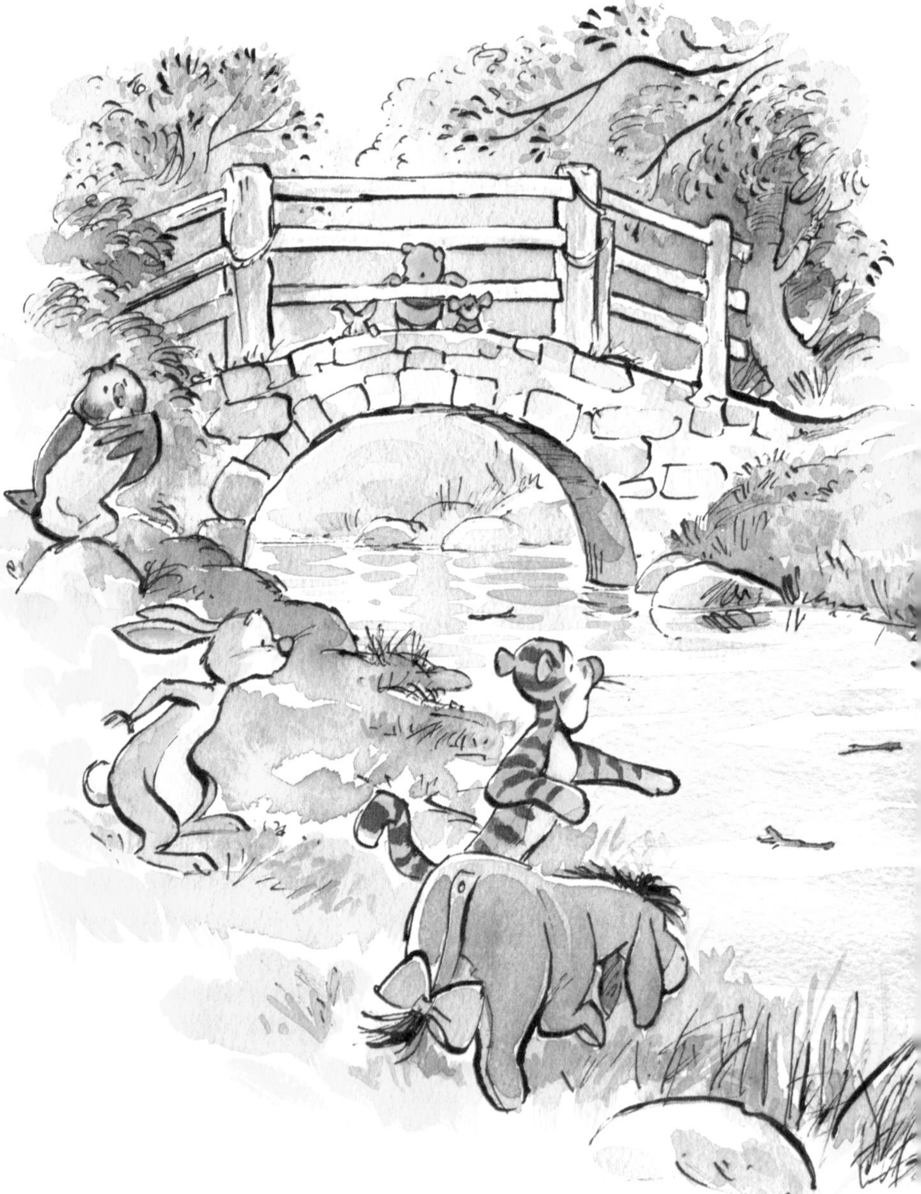

"You're questing for something small?
Pooh Sticks are small. And they end up
in unexpected places, too."

"Good point, Donkey Boy. We'd better
have a game, just in case!"

Keep playing with the joy of a child all your life,
and you'll never be truly old.

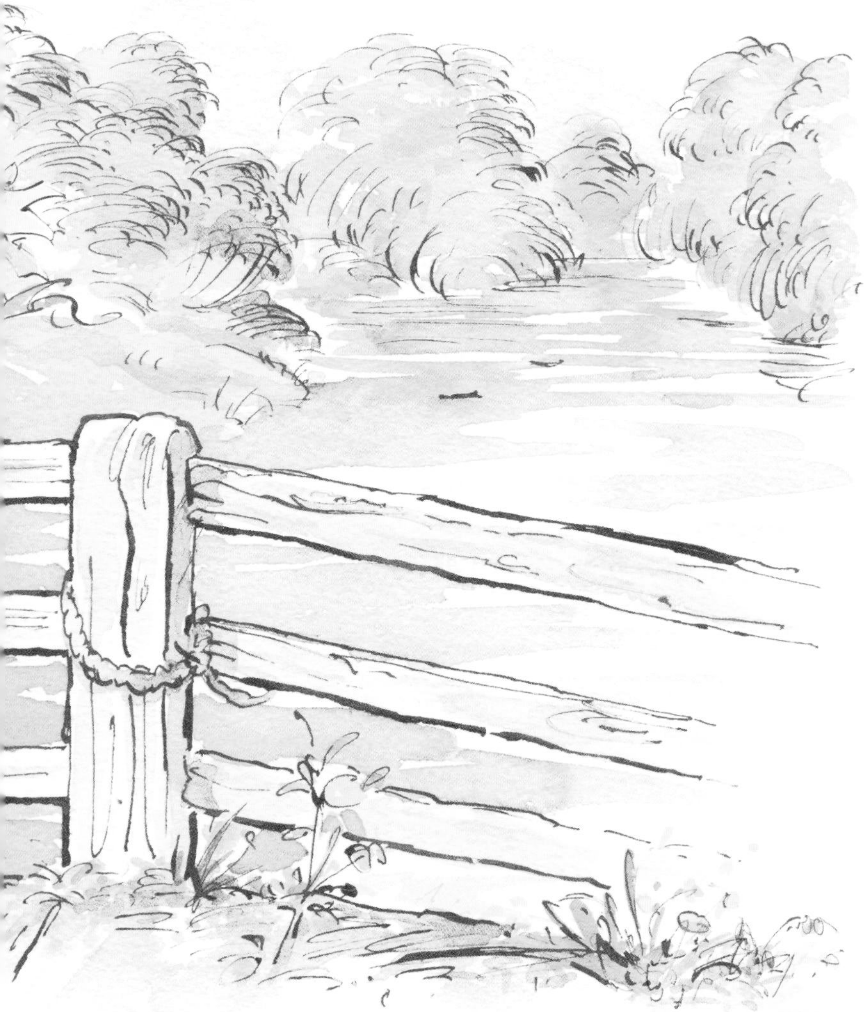

"It's getting dark!
    Where will we sleep?"

"You can stay at my place if you like. It's not much, but what it lacks in charm it makes up for in dampness."

"The hand that gives, gathers."
    —British proverb

"Thank you for sharing your house, Eeyore."

"You're welcome, Pooh. It may be a bit cramped, but I will say I've never been warmer."

Avoid hurting others' feelings whenever possible.

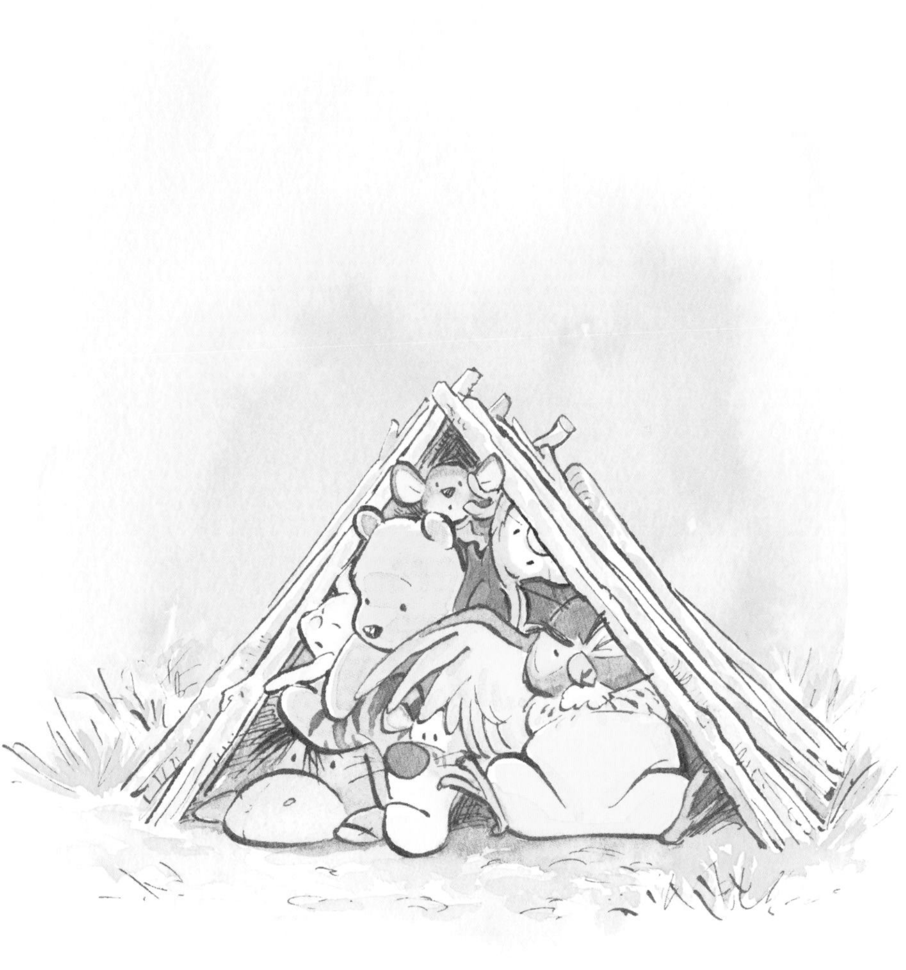

"Then again, it might be nearly as lovely to sleep out under the stars."

Be flexible and creative, and you can overcome nearly anything!

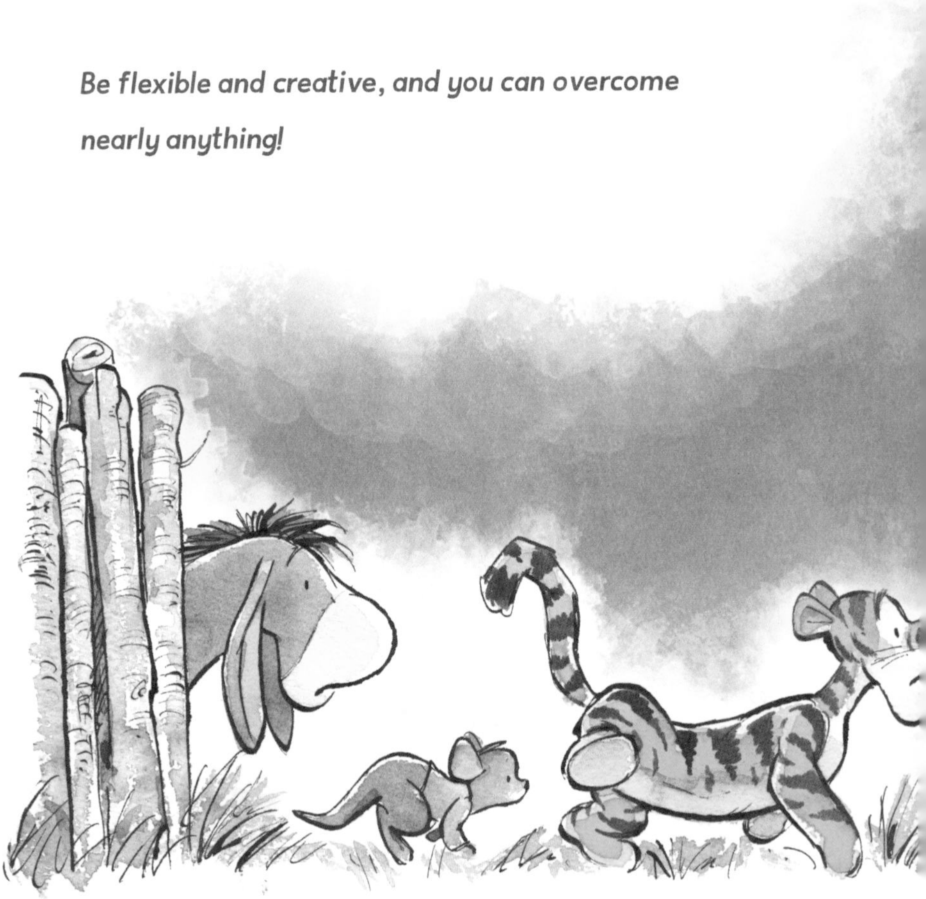

"Look at that full moon!"

"Full of what, Owl?"

"Er, funny you should ask, Pooh.
I'll have to look that up once I'm back
with my books and learned papers."

Even the wise don't know everything.

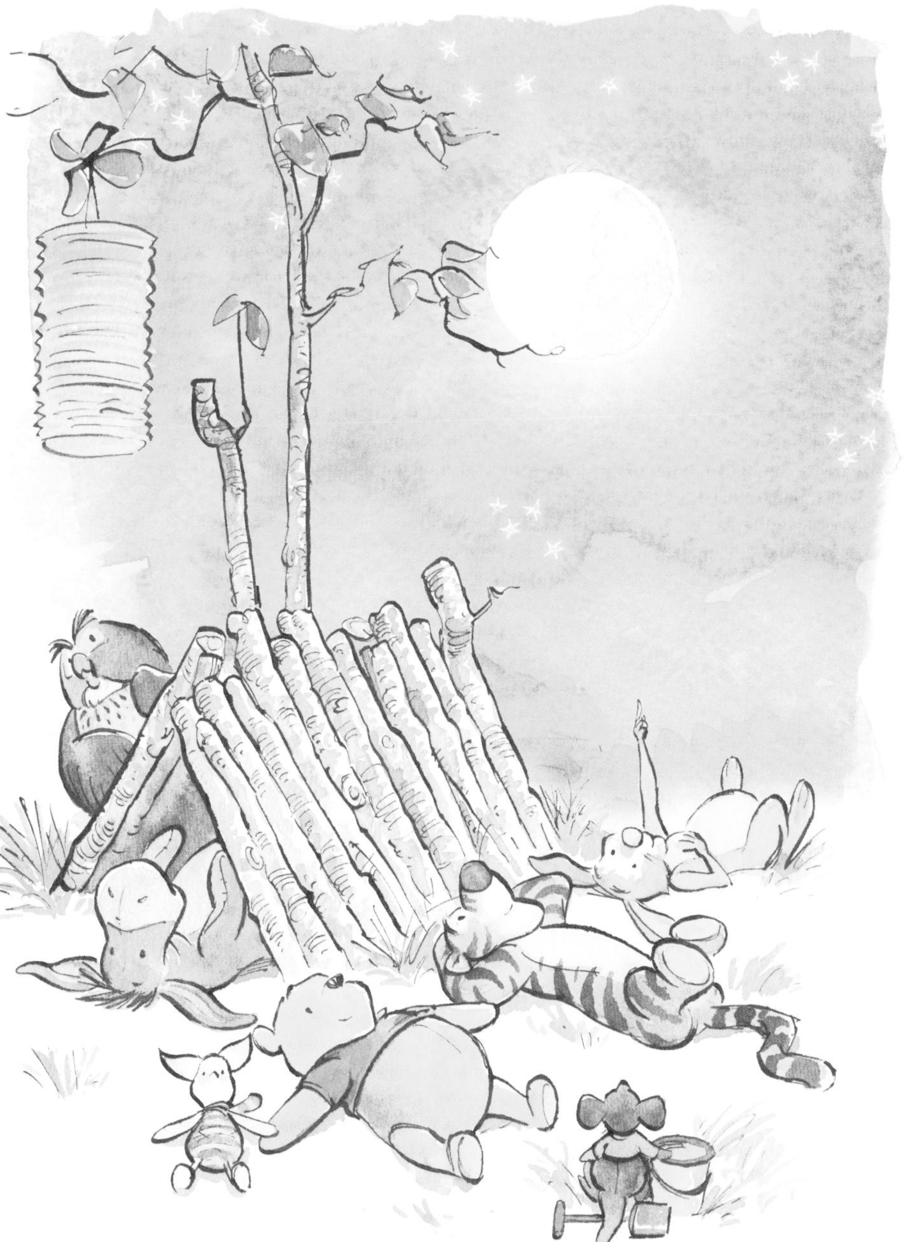

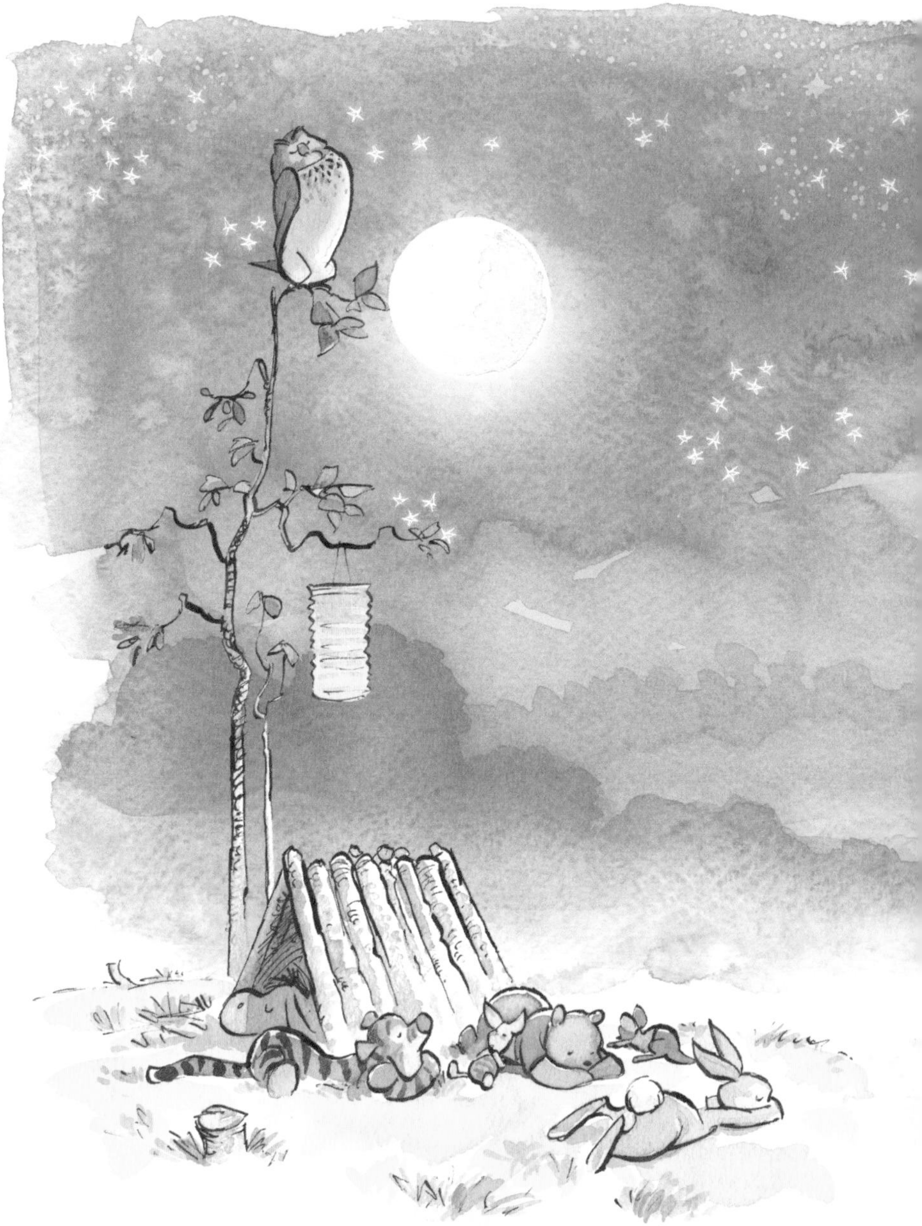

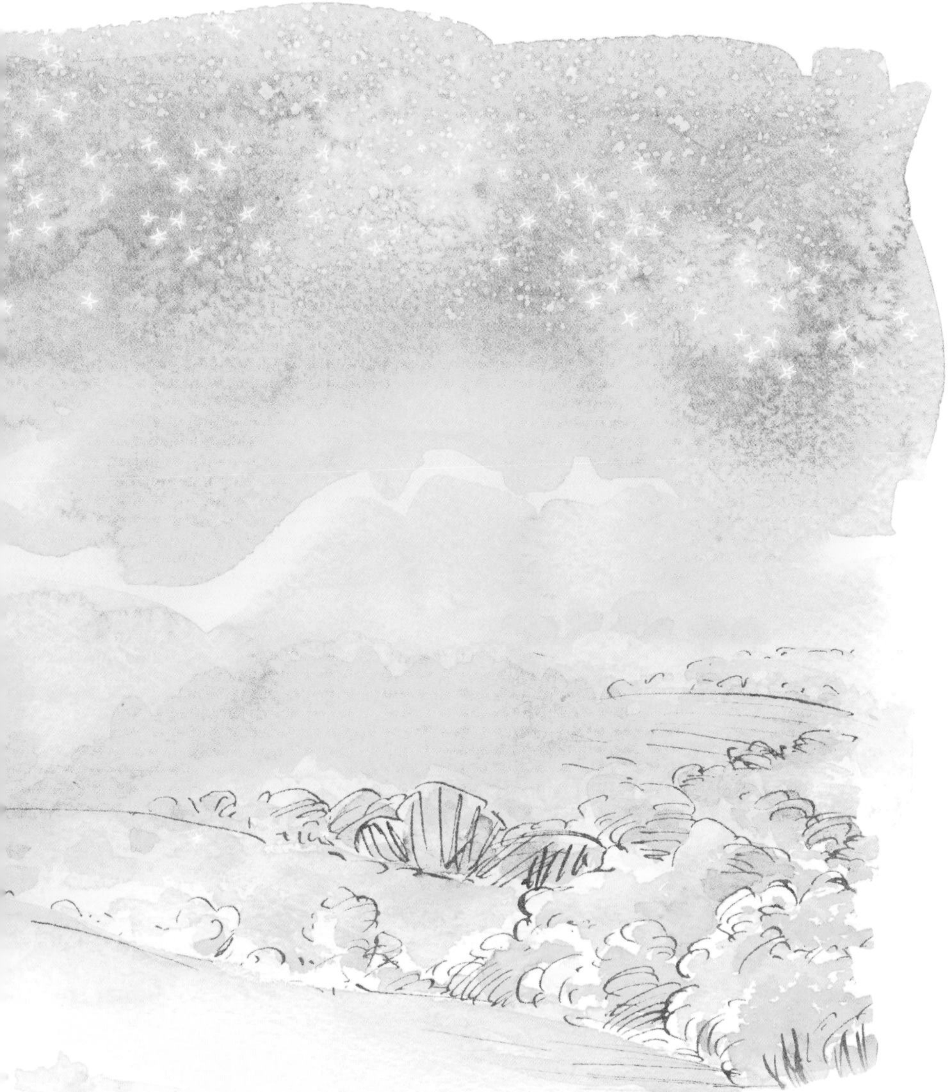

"Oh, d-d-dear. Did you hear a sound, Pooh?"

"Yes. Take my hand, Piglet, and perhaps it will feel less scary for both of us."

When fears are shared, they can seem less frightening.

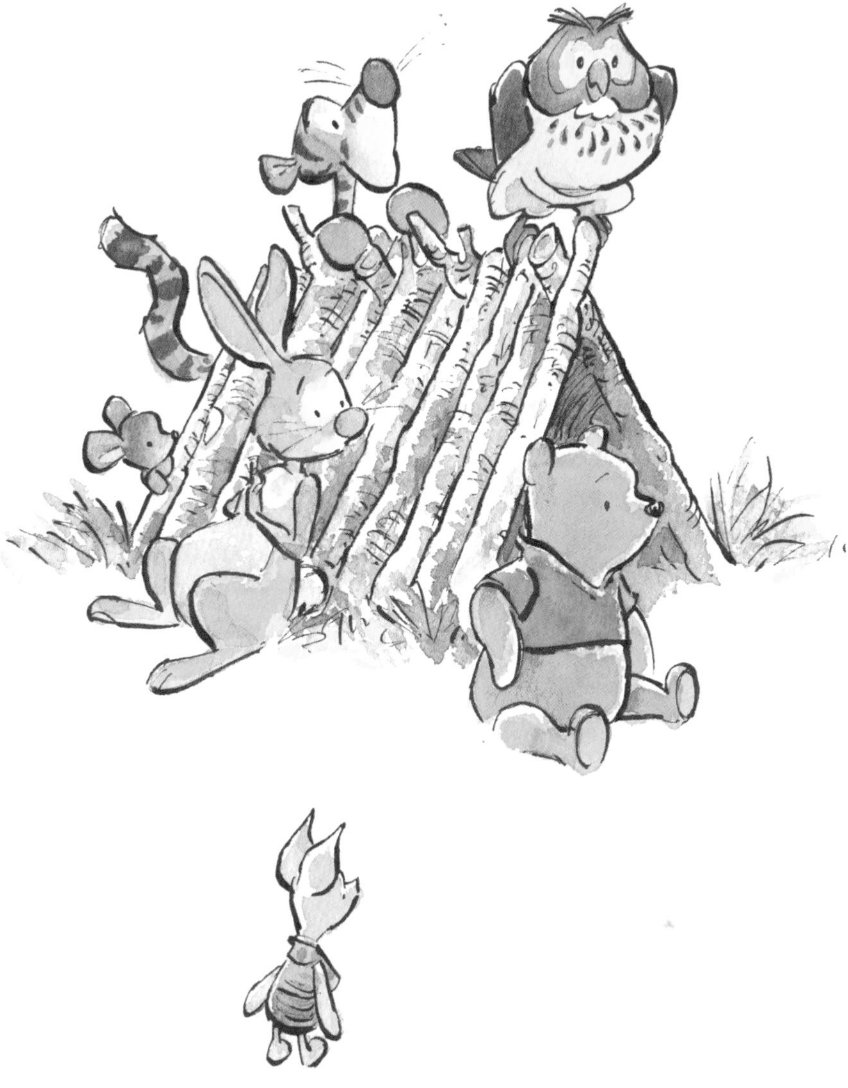

"No sense questing on an empty stomach. What's for breakfast?"

"All I have is this thistle I was saving for myself. But I s'pose we could share."

"Er, thanks, Eeyore. But I have a better idea. Follow me."

The best things in life are not those you keep, but those you share.

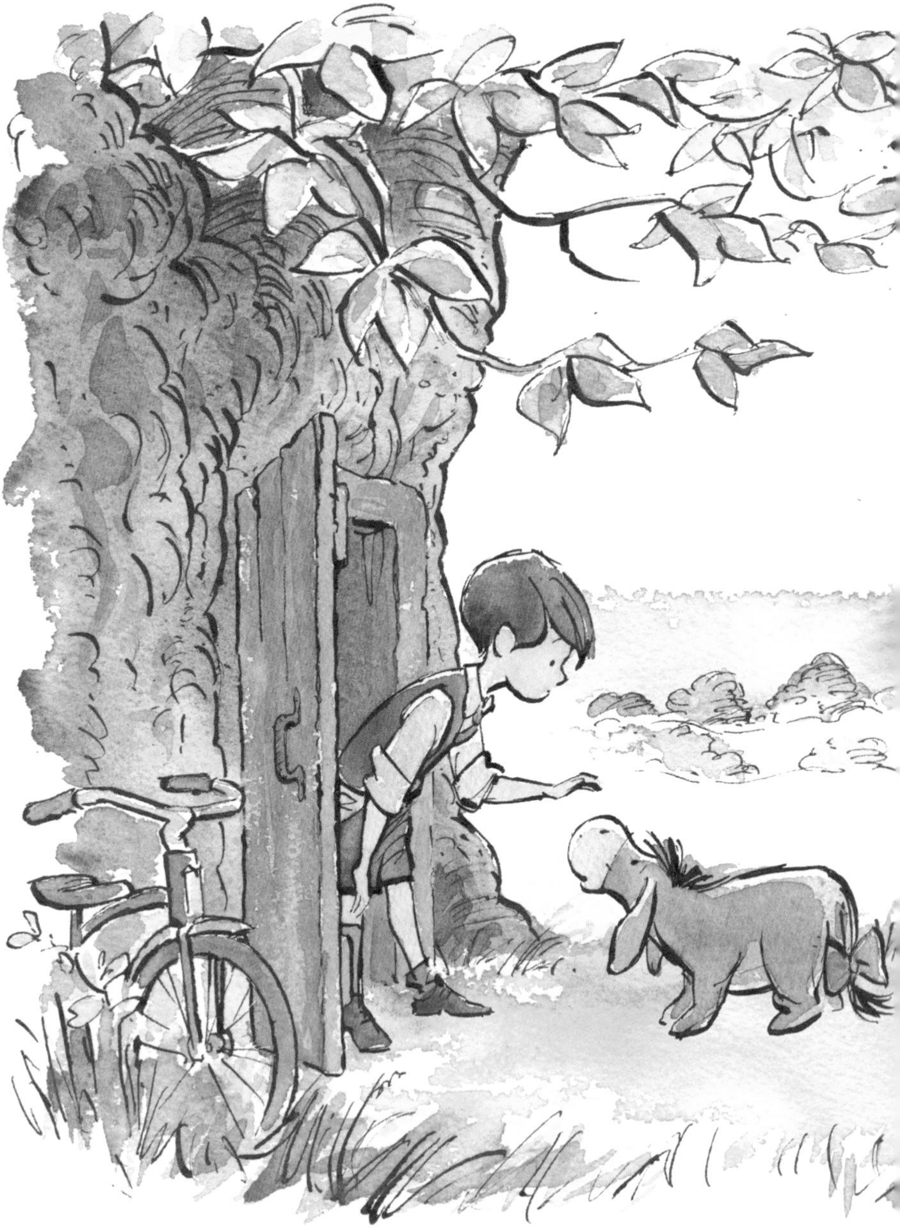

"Hullo, everyone! You've been on a quest, you say? Please come in and tell me all about it over breakfast."

Allow yourself to be surprised—
especially by happiness, friendship, and kindness.

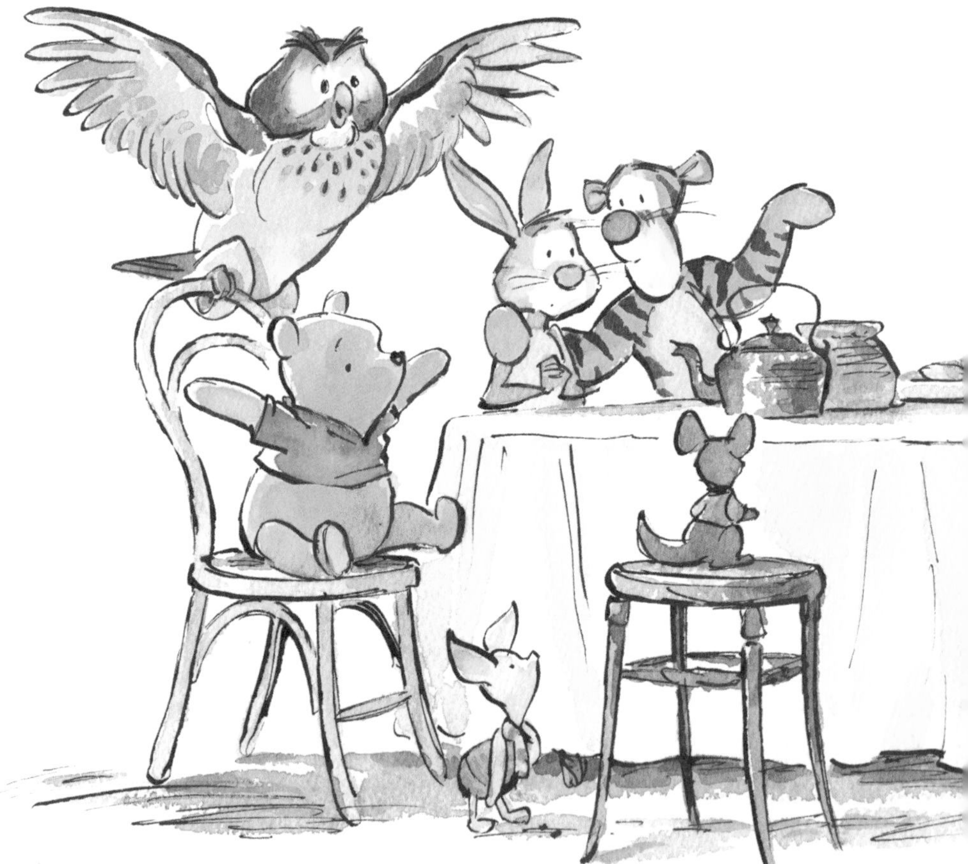

"What a magnificent adventure! And what wonderful friends for trying to help find my lucky stone!"

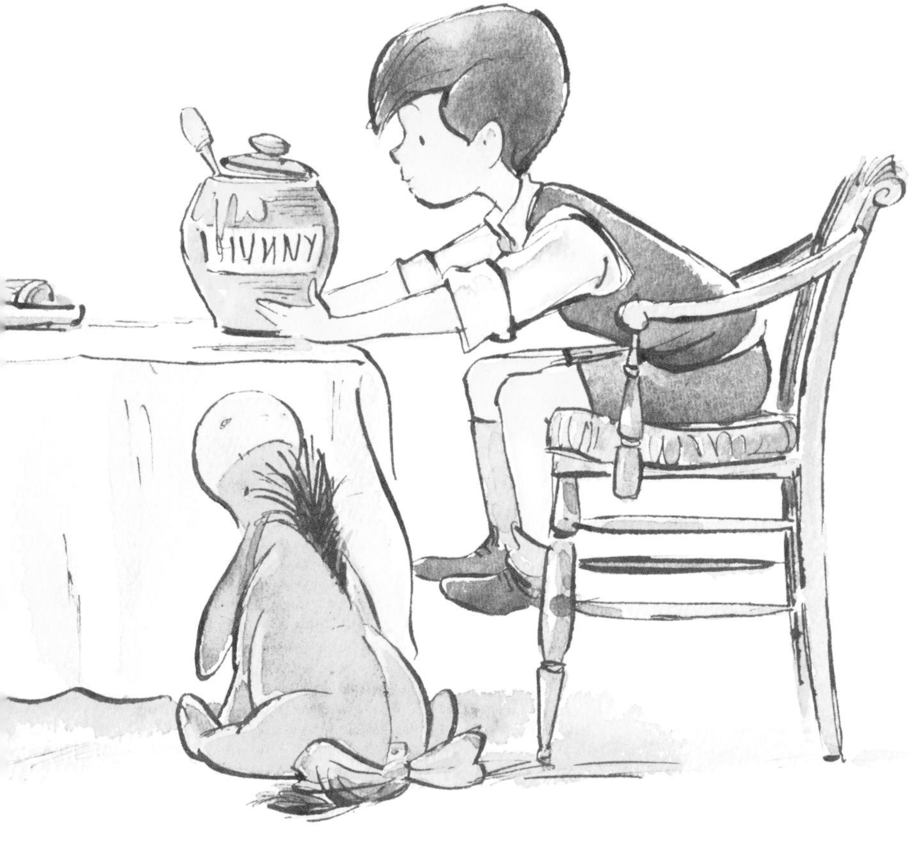
HUNNY

A memory shines more brightly when it's shared.

"But we didn't find it in the end."

"That's because my lucky stone wasn't really lost, Pooh Bear. When I reached into my pocket this morning, there it was!"

Even when it's difficult, try your best to be truthful with your friends.

"Looks like an ordinary stone to me. What's so special about it?"

"Well, you see, Eeyore, I found this stone on the very same day I first met Pooh Bear. It reminds me how lucky I am to have a friend like Pooh—and all the rest of you, too!"

Even the simplest of objects can have great value,
not for themselves but for the memories they hold.

"Hooray for lucky stones! And for quests!"

"Even though I had the thing you were questing for all along?"

There's no bad excuse for a party!

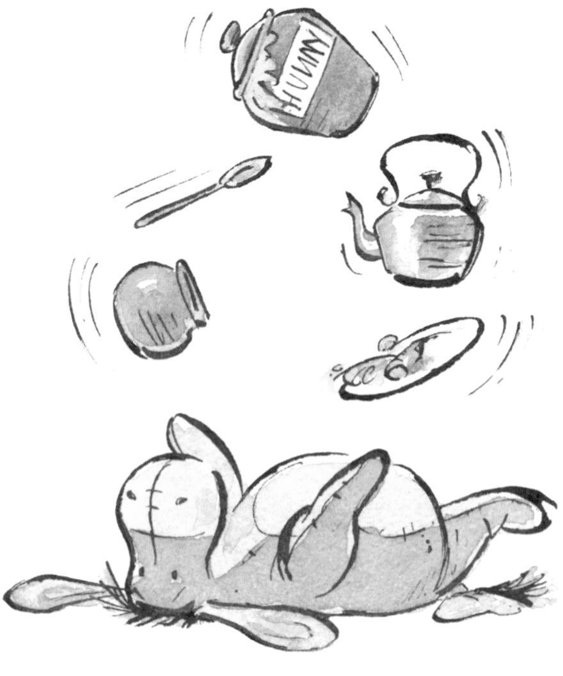
HUNNY

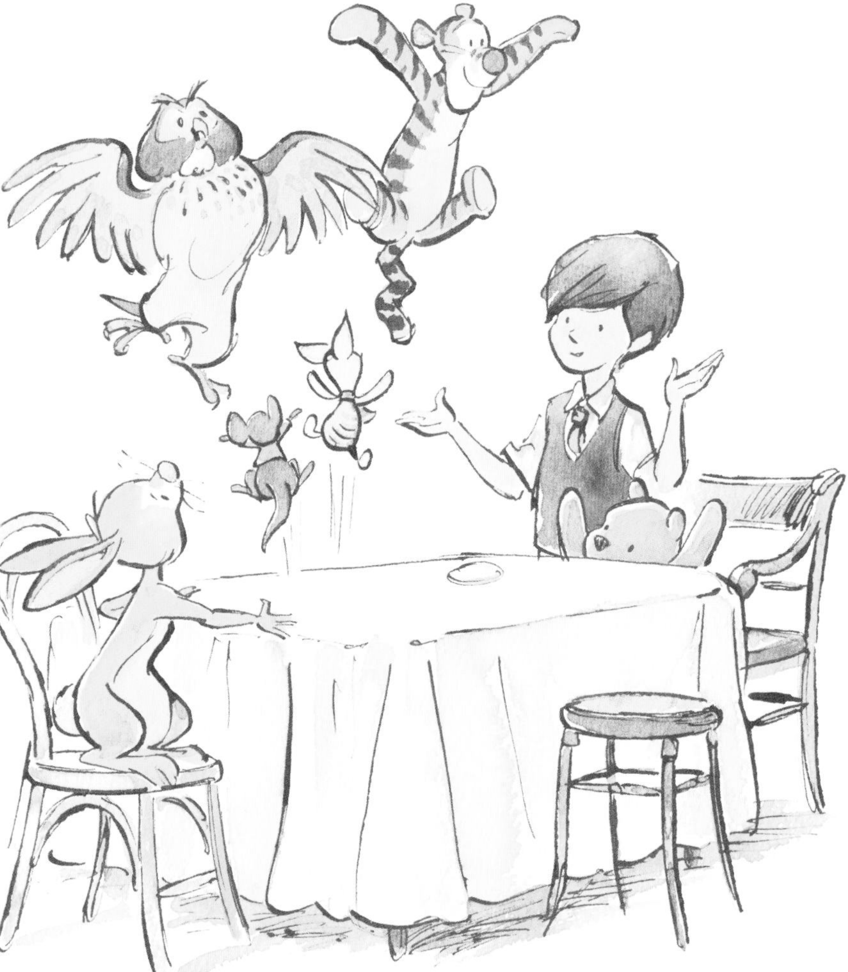

"True, we weren't sure exactly what we were doing or where we were going, and some difficult things happened. But we had some adventures, and we did it all together."

Allow yourself to be open to the journey.

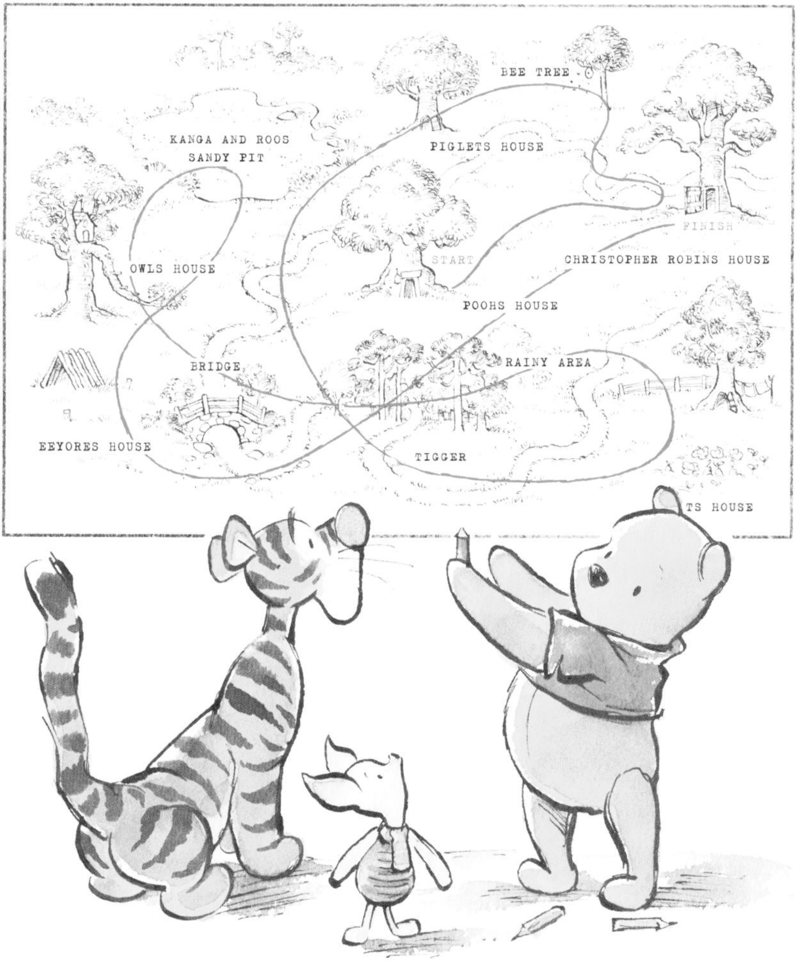
BEE TREE
KANGA AND ROOS
SANDY PIT
PIGLETS HOUSE
FINISH
START
OWLS HOUSE
CHRISTOPHER ROBINS HOUSE
POOHS HOUSE
BRIDGE
RAINY AREA
EEYORES HOUSE
TIGGER
TS HOUSE

"But you spent an entire day on
   the quest!"

"And what more pleasant way to
   spend a day than with friends,
   trying to help another friend?"

Savor the little things in life—because someday you may realize they were the biggest things of all.

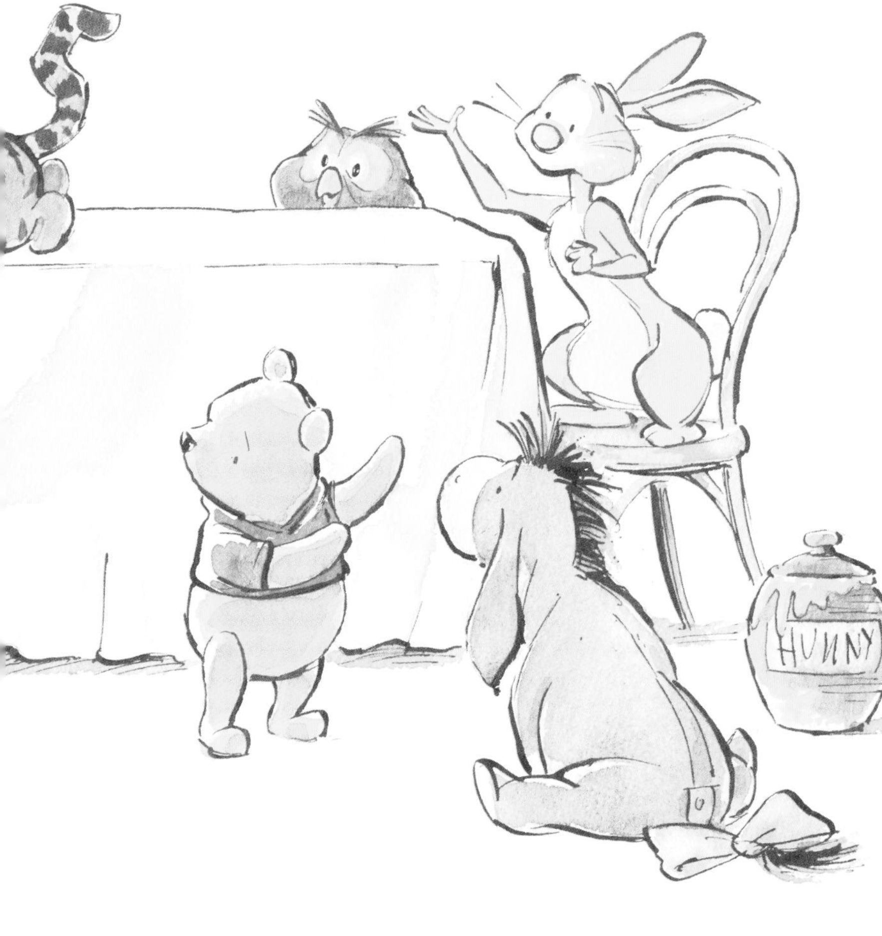
HUNNY

"Silly old bear!"

The End

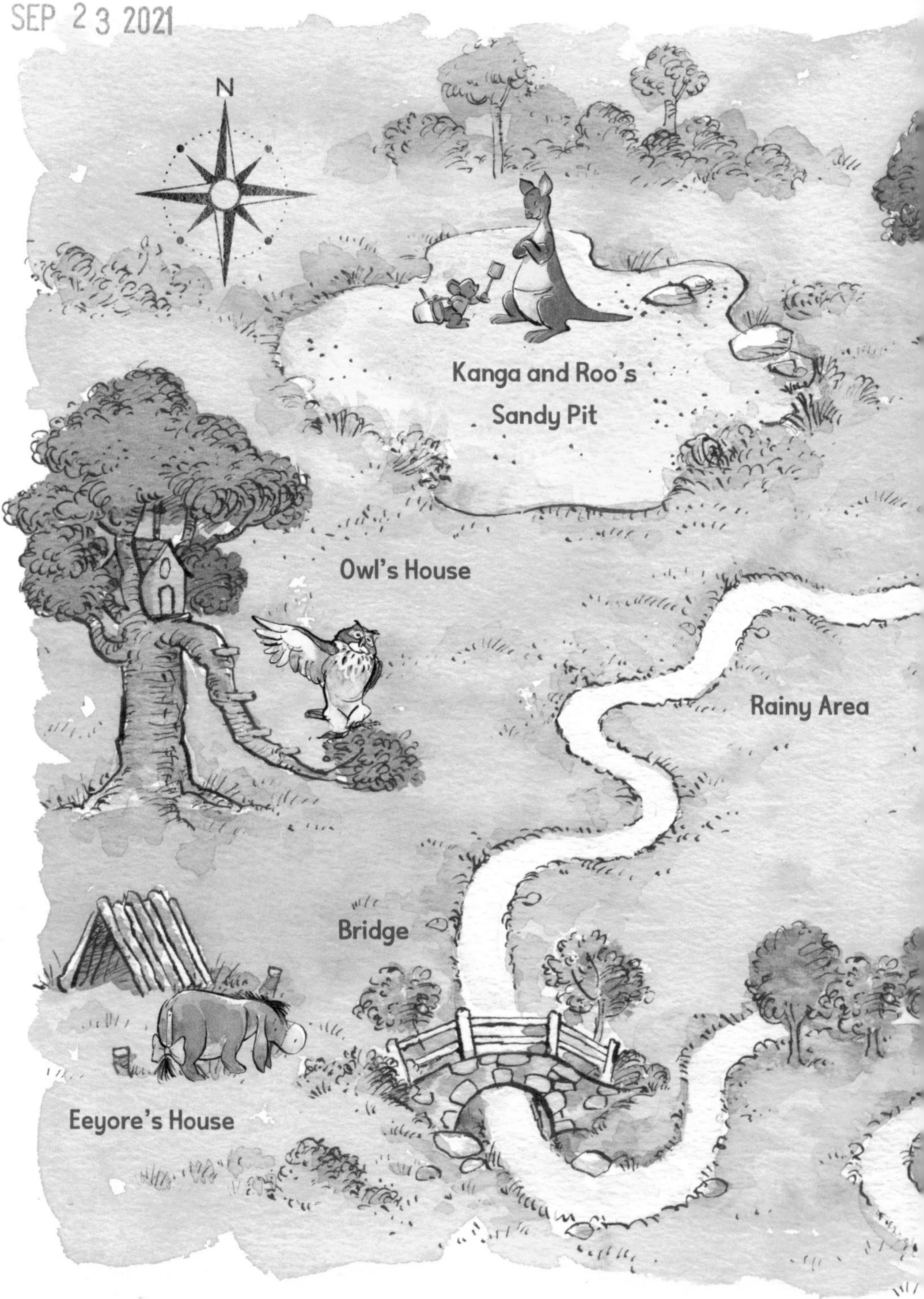
N
Kanga and Roo's
Sandy Pit
Owl's House
Rainy Area
Bridge
Eeyore's House